Praise for *It Happened One Night*

"Mizejewski is marvelously alert to the romance, sex, class feeling and star power that made *It Happened One Night* a landmark comedy. An indispensable guide to what "It" is all about."

Maria DiBattista, Princeton University

"Linda Mizejewski's *It Happened One Night*, like Frank Capra's, is tough-minded and tender, politically and discursively astute, yet open to the humor and mystery of "young people in love." Her command of the scholarship is impressive, her prose is nimble and sharp. A landmark study of a landmark film."

Leland Poague, Iowa State University

"What a wonderful read! Mizejewski's witty and lucid study of *It Happened One Night* offers a knowledgeable introduction not only to this important film but to the genre of romantic comedy and the scholarship it has inspired."

Kathleen Rowe Karlyn, University of Oregon

T0307859

Wiley-Blackwell Studies in Film and Television
Series Editors: Diane Negra and Yvonne Tasker

Experienced media studies teachers know that real breakthroughs in the classroom are often triggered by texts that an austere notion of the canon would disqualify. Unlike other short book series, *Wiley-Blackwell Studies in Film and Television* works from a broad field of prospective film and television programs, selected less for their adherence to definitions of "art" than for their resonance with audiences.

From *Top Hat* to *Hairspray*, from early sitcoms to contemporary forensic dramas, the series encompasses a range of film and television material that reflects diverse genres, forms, styles and periods. The texts explored here are known and recognized world-wide for their ability to generate discussion and debate about evolving media industries as well as, crucially, representations and conceptualizations of gender, class, citizenship, race, consumerism and capitalism, and other facets of identity and experience. This series is designed to communicate these themes clearly and effectively to media studies students at all levels while also introducing groundbreaking scholarship of the very highest caliber. These are the films and shows we really want to watch, the new "teachable canon" of alternative classics that range from silent film to *CSI*.

IT HAPPENED ONE NIGHT
NIGHT
LINDA MIZEJEWSKI

A John Wiley & Sons, Ltd., Publication

This edition first published 2010
Copyright © Linda Mizejewski 2010

Blackwell Publishing was acquired by John Wiley & Sons in February 2007. Blackwell's publishing program has been merged with Wiley's global Scientific, Technical, and Medical business to form Wiley-Blackwell.

Registered Office
John Wiley & Sons Ltd, The Atrium, Southern Gate, Chichester, West Sussex, PO19 8SQ, United Kingdom

Editorial Offices
350 Main Street, Malden, MA 02148-5020, USA
9600 Garsington Road, Oxford, OX4 2DQ, UK
The Atrium, Southern Gate, Chichester, West Sussex, PO19 8SQ, UK

For details of our global editorial offices, for customer services, and for information about how to apply for permission to reuse the copyright material in this book please see our website at www.wiley.com/wiley-blackwell.

The right of Linda Mizejewski to be identified as the author of this work has been asserted in accordance with the Copyright, Designs and Patents Act 1988.

Library of Congress Cataloging-in-Publication Data

Mizejewski, Linda.
It happened one night / Linda Mizejewski.
   p.   cm. – (Wiley-Blackwell studies in film and television)
Includes bibliographical references and index.
ISBN 978-1-4051-7389-6 (hardcover : alk. paper) – ISBN 978-1-4051-7388-9 (pbk. : alk. paper) 1.   It happened one night (Motion picture) I.   Title.
PN1997.I755M59 2009
791.43′72–dc22

                                                            2009010789

A catalogue record for this book is available from the British Library.

Set in 10.5/13pt Minion by SPi Publisher Services, Pondicherry, India
Printed and bound in Singapore by Fabulous Printers Pte Ltd

001   2010

For George, with romance and comedy

Contents

List of Illustrations

Acknowledgments

This book started and ended with the interest, advice, and inspiration of Diane Negra and Yvonne Tasker, the series editors for this project, who were always on top of things and made the work a lot of fun. My thanks also goes to Jayne Fargnoli and Margot A. Morse at Wiley-Blackwell for spoiling me with their quick responses to all my questions. In addition, I'm grateful to Walter Biggins at the University of Mississippi Press, who allowed me early access to Bernard F. Dick's biography of Claudette Colbert. At the Ohio State University, I was lucky to have the research assistance of movie-loving Libby Zay, an enthusiastic student in Women's Studies, as well as a grant-in-aid from the College of the Arts and Humanities. At home, I was lucky to have the support of George Bauman, ever passionate about writing and romantic movies.

Introduction
Little Picture, Big Classic

Legends and a Legendary Hit

It Happened One Night (1934) opens with tycoon Alexander Andrews (Walter Connolly) outraged to hear that his daughter Ellie (Claudette Colbert) is refusing to eat the food sent to her cabin on the yacht. "Well, why don't you jam it down her throat?" he demands of the chief steward. "Well, it's not as simple as all that," the steward ruefully replies.

The steward is right. The daughter is not a child but a married woman, and the power struggle involves far more than physical force. A sleeper hit from a small studio, *It Happened One Night* is deceptively simple in other ways as well. In the 1930s, its audiences recognized it as a "bus story" of the type popular at the time, about two strangers meeting and falling in love over the course of a journey. In the script, Peter Warne (Clark Gable), the film's romantic hero, describes it as "a simple story for simple people." The settings are modest. Though it opens on a yacht, most of the action takes place on or around a Greyhound bus and dusty back roads. Because of this simplicity, Claudette Colbert reported her grave doubts, during the shooting, about the likelihood of the film's success. Depression-era audiences wanted glamour from Hollywood, she said, "And here we were, looking a little seedy, riding our bus" (McBride, 1992: 307). Indeed, Colbert had only three changes of clothing in the entire film, and production values were not high. The most famous prop in this film is a blanket, and the film's implied star endorsement was that real men do not wear undershirts, a revelation made when Peter removes his shirt to reveal a bare chest in a key scene.

The place of *It Happened One Night* in film history is likewise reckoned to be straightforward. The film captivated Hollywood in the 1930s, inspired the genre of romantic comedy, turned "poverty row" Columbia Pictures into a major studio, and made Gable the top leading man of the decade. The name of its director, Frank Capra, has become short-hand for American populist cinema, with *It Happened One Night* as the prototype of the "Capraesque" film, which portrays the erosion of class difference and the triumph of the ordinary citizen.

Yet as the steward says, it's not as simple as all that. Even the opening conversation of *It Happened One Night*, with its questions of power, need, and desire, resonate with the irony of wealthy people arguing about a hunger strike in the middle of the Depression. Likewise, the simple blanket and missing undershirt suggest both the gritty materiality and social enormity of what is at stake – bedding and skin, class and sex – in a movie set in an era when many Americans went hungry. Capra's politics, Gable's stardom, the development of Columbia Pictures, the meanings of this film in the Depression, and the implications for romantic comedy are complicated topics crisscrossed by contending histories. The aim of this book is to unpack these questions and themes and to map out the debates, contexts, and controversies that make *It Happened One Night* a key text for the history of cinema and for cultural studies.

Without dispute, *It Happened One Night* is the boilerplate for Hollywood's favorite way of constructing the heterosexual couple. Its formula of the quarreling duo, spunky heroine, romantic triangle, and class/cultural conflict continues to dominate the genre of romantic comedy, easily making the transition into the twenty-first century. Undisputed, too, is the film's status as a runaway hit. Breaking box office records on its initial release, it was the first film to sweep the Academy Awards, winning Best Picture, Best Director, Best Screenplay, Best Actor, and Best Actress – a feat equaled only twice later in the twentieth century. It was also one of only five comedies in that century to win the Academy Award for Best Picture.[1] Even in the early

Peter and Ellie begin to break down the famous "walls of Jericho" in a publicity shot for *It Happened One Night*. Courtesy of Photofest.

years of the Awards, the trend was for the big honors to go to the big pictures, usually to ambitious epics or tragedies – in the 1930s, the historical dramas *All Quiet on the Western Front* (1930), *Cimarron* (1931), and *Cavalcade* (1933) and the social melodrama *Grand Hotel* (1932). In this context, the sweep of an unpretentious comedy from a minor studio was all the more extraordinary.

Yet the big topic of *It Happened One Night* is no less than the way we imagine and fantasize marriage and heterosexuality, a topic that still sweeps us up in its emotional impact. The romantic comedy has emerged as one of our primary cultural stories of heterosexuality, and the ongoing influence of *It Happened One Night* speaks to the weight of this particular picturing of the couple: cantankerous, willful, needful of lessons about compromise and love.

The plot begins with the rebellion of heiress Ellen (Ellie) Andrews against her father, who objects to her secret marriage to the wealthy King Westley (Jameson Thomas). Mr. Andrews despises Westley as a "fake," so he has virtually kidnapped his daughter and confined her to his yacht in Florida, preventing her from joining her husband in New York to consummate the marriage. Ellie makes a bold escape by jumping overboard and sneaking aboard a Greyhound bus to head north and reunite with her husband. Spoiled and sheltered, Ellie makes a hapless traveler, but on the bus she meets reporter Peter, who has just lost his job on a newspaper. Despite his contempt for the wealthy Ellie, Peter offers to get her to New York so he can scoop the story – runaway heiress! – and regain his job.

The journey of Ellie and Peter from Florida to New York takes place over three days but, more importantly, three nights that mark the milestones in their relationship. On the first night, the bus is stranded and, for lack of money, they are forced to spend the night in the same motel room. In a scene that has become iconic in film history, Peter hangs a blanket between the beds – the "walls of Jericho" as he archly calls it – to preserve their respectability, modesty, and – quite frankly – Ellie's virginity. On the second night of their travels, they flee the bus because Ellie has been recognized by one of the passengers, and they sleep in a hayfield, isolated under the stars and aware of their growing attraction to each other. The third night, however, marks the turning point of the story. Again sharing a motel room separated by a blanket, they are only a few hours from New York and Ellie's return to her husband. Both are obviously depressed about this. In a shocking moment, Ellie leaves her bed, pulls aside the blanket, goes to Peter's bed, and declares her love for him. Audiences in 1934 must have gasped.

What follows is a melee of the kind of confusion and misunderstandings that have become staples of the romantic comedy film. Peter realizes he cannot marry Ellie in his penniless state, so he steals away to New York to write up the new scoop – heiress decides to marry journalist! – intending to be back before Ellen wakes up. Instead, Ellie awakes to find him gone, assumes she's been abandoned, and sadly arranges to reunite with her father and husband. She also stalls the consummation of the marriage, insisting on a huge society wedding. Angry and broken-hearted, Peter makes an appointment with Mr. Andrews to ask for money – not the $10,000 reward being offered, but the $39.60 he has spent on Ellie during their journey. Mr. Andrews, unhappily resigned to having King Westley for a son-in-law, realizes that Peter is the man who can make Ellie happy. As he escorts his daughter down the aisle at the elegant outdoor wedding, he whispers to her that he's arranged for a getaway car if she wants to make her escape.

The wedding ceremony begins, but when the minister poses the ritual question to Ellie – "Wilt thou take this man …" – she hesitates for just a moment and then bolts from the altar, the newsreel cameras following her flight through the crowds and across the lawn. Her spectacular veil and wedding-dress train trailing behind her, Ellie escapes propriety and opts for true love – the first of many cinematic runaway brides. In the next scene, we see Mr. Andrews happily and tipsily arranging for a pay-off to King Westley and an annulment of Westley's marriage to Ellie. The film's penultimate shot shows a puzzled older couple who have rented a tourist cottage in Michigan to some newly-weds. The newly-weds have oddly requested a toy trumpet and a blanket, despite the hot night. In the famous final shot of *It Happened One Night*, no human figures appear in the frame. We hear a tinny trumpet being blown, and we see the edge of a blanket falling to the floor, one of Hollywood's most clever euphemisms for everything that could not appear on the screen: sex, the wedding night, loss of virginity, nudity, carnal passion.

Sex, romance, adventure, a rich girl who slums it to find love – little wonder this film enthralled 1934 audiences and continues to charm us. In addition to its love story, it echoes many of Western culture's most familiar tales and tropes. *It Happened One Night* is structured like a fairy tale. Over the course of three magical nights, the princess is rescued from the "bad" king, King Westley, by the jaunty hero who is secret heir to a different kind of richness – integrity and love – played by "King Gable, a king of the people" (Maltby, 1998: 151). Peter is in fact hailed as a "king" by rowdy drunks early in the film. This suggests yet another ancient pattern – the topsy-turvy world of the carnival, where crazy reversals take place – the unemployed drunk crowned king, the princess wooed by the pauper. The story's journey from innocence to experience also characterizes it as an archetypal tale of initiation, and its form as a comedy guarantees the subversion of the old guard by a new generation, the overthrowing of the stodgy world of the father for the newer, better world of the young couple.

Along with these large-scale themes, *It Happened One Night* draws us into very specific gender politics and cultural issues. The wayward heroine is a version of the 1920s New Woman who smokes cigarettes and who, as Elizabeth Kendall (1990: 49) puts it, chooses sex over status. As a feminist text, the story is structured by female desire fueling two daring escapes, first from a tyrannical father and then from the tyrannies of high society. As American folklore, these escapes place Ellie with the likes of Huck Finn and Holden Caulfield, rebels and dropouts seeking a more authentic life. The specific escape to Michigan for the elopement and honeymoon takes the couple into Ernest Hemingway territory. By the 1930s, his Nick Adams stories had staked out the Michigan woods as the sanctuary from personal and social disappointments. The fact that we never actually *see* this couple in the woods places the film in the tradition of American romanticism, the fantasy of "a visionary community that has no social reality," as one critic puts it (Carney, 1996: 261). *It Happened One Night* also works as a Depression-era fable, pooh-poohing the wealthy and celebrating the down-and-out crowd on the Greyhound bus. Its American political fable unites the heiress with Everyman, a couple signifying the elision of class difference and the embrace of middle-class, down-to-earth stability. Finally, the relationship of Ellie and Peter in *It Happened One Night* has been touted as an example of the egalitarian marriage model that had developed in the United States in the 1920s and which remains an attractive ideal.

Adaptation: "Night Bus" to Sleeper Hit

Yet this film's positions on class, female independence, marriage, and relationships between the sexes have all been hotly contested by critics in debates that remain intriguingly unsettled, as the following chapters explain. The class and gender issues are evident in the changes made in the adaptation of *It Happened One Night* from "Night Bus." A 1933 short story by Samuel Hopkins Adams which originally appeared in *Cosmopolitan* magazine and was published the following year in a 10-cent Dell "Vestpocket" edition (Dick, 2008: 77), "Night Bus" was a popular and widely circulated story. The film adaptation follows the basic structure of the original: the runaway heiress, the meeting with Peter on the bus, Peter's refusal to accept the $10,000 reward from Mr. Andrews in New York, and the heroine's choice of Peter over the wealthy King Westley. However, in the Adams story the class difference between the main characters is minimal. Elspeth is an heiress, but Peter went to college with her cousin, implying an upper-class background. A chemist and would-be inventor, Peter makes a point about how little money he earns in comparison to her fortune, but he is far from the flat-broke reporter in the Capra film.

Even more striking is the difference between the story's sexually sophisticated Elspeth and the film version's virginal Ellie. "Night Bus" was pitched at popular fiction readers who, since the 1920s, expected a worldly, independent heroine, enjoying new freedoms, meeting a middle-class man whose imagination would win her heart (Sklar, 1998: 41). Confident and perhaps sexually experienced, Elspeth shows no squeamishness about sharing motel rooms with Peter, though the story makes clear that they are in separate beds divided by the "walls of Jericho." Not yet married to Westley, she intends to rendezvous with him in New York. But by the time she and Peter get there, Westley is no longer of interest to her, and she pursues Peter shamelessly. First she sends him a toy trumpet in the mail, and then she appears at his apartment to make certain he knows what it means. "Would you like to kiss me, Peter?" she asks (Adams ([1933] 1979: 90). As Robert Sklar has remarked, this sexual aggression and the story's "link between Elspeth's independent will and the possibility of sexual license" is unusual even for the era's popular fiction featuring the mobile New Woman (1998: 42).

Elspeth is assertive and resourceful in the Adams story. Traveling with Peter, she uses her power of persuasion to barter for food and for shelter. When they need to cross a turbulent river in a leaky boat, she helps with the rowing and bailing, proving herself a tough sailor. This is in sharp contrast to Ellie in *It Happened One Night*, who is carried by Peter across the water and who during the journey becomes totally dependent on him for money and protection, wailing in panic when she thinks he has deserted her. The cinematic Ellie is far more sheltered and impractical than the short story's Elspeth. Noting the changes from story to film, Sidney Gottlieb argues that Ellie has been transformed from an active, independent heroine to "an immobile romantic idol … a dreamy vision of a beautiful woman … a man's idealized love object" (1988: 133, 134). Gottlieb borrows from feminist film criticism the charge that Hollywood cinema's male gaze fetishizes the female body and relegates women to passive figures in narratives controlled by male agency.

The question of agency in this film is complicated and not entirely explained through this visual theory of men as spectators and women as objects of their gaze. But the visual cinematic production of Ellie certainly pictures her as smaller and more defenseless than the character of Elspeth on which she was based. Even though Claudette Colbert appears in most of the movie in a modest traveling outfit, her femininity is heightened by the frequent use of soft-focus close-ups and by hazy backlighting which transforms her into an "immobile romantic idol." This combination of lighting and soft focus is used, for example, when she stands outside the bus smoking during the scene where her suitcase is stolen, in the first motel scene when she looks out of the window at the rain, and extensively in the scene where she and Peter sleep in the hayfield. In addition, the framing emphasizes sexual difference by foregrounding Ellie's petite build on several occasions. When she stands facing Peter just after he has erected the "walls of Jericho," her vulnerability is evident in their relative sizes. For viewers who missed this, Peter approvingly says, "You're kinda little, aren't ya," as he helps her into his bathrobe the next morning. Later, he easily lifts her over his shoulder to carry her across the stream.

The point is that while both the short story and the film feature a spirited modern heroine, *It Happened One Night* produces a far more contradictory one through the codes of Hollywood cinema. The cinematic character Ellie makes more dramatic and defiant gestures than Elspeth – diving off the boat, approaching Peter's bed, and running away from her grand wedding – all of which make good Hollywood scenes. But Ellie is often scripted into a submissive and traditional feminine role and pictured by the cinematic devices that produce the romantic idol rather than the liberated woman. These changes in character coding (which are explained in detail in chapter 2) are related to the difference in sexual tone between the film and the short story, which construct heterosexual desire in very different ways. The adaptation process is always a cultural register signaling how gender and sexuality, among other things, can be imagined and produced in different mediums at particular historical moments. The star image and performances of Claudette Colbert and Clark Gable are additional key elements of the adaptation which generate very specific ideas of gender and sexuality (discussed in chapter 4).

According to Capra's autobiography, he found and read "Night Bus" at a barbershop and liked it because it "had the smell of novelty" (1971: 178). Capra's previous films had included the successful melodramas *Ladies of Leisure* (1930), *The Miracle Woman* (1931), *Forbidden* (1932), and *The Bitter Tea of General Yen* (1933), all of which featured defiant, impassioned women who suffer for their choices. The "novelty" of "Night Bus" for Capra may have been the happy ending for such a heroine. As Sklar points out, *It Happened One Night* is Capra's first film "featuring a rich woman of independent will who is not punished because she accepts the yoke of the genteel hero's imagination" (1998: 45). The significance of this is the difference between melodrama and comedy for female pleasure and agency, as Kathleen Rowe (1995: 112–14) has argued.

Early versions of the script were turned down by A-list actresses Miriam Hopkins, Margaret Sullavan, and Constance Bennett. Capra claims that the successful script revision – his collaboration with scriptwriter Robert Riskin – followed the advice of his story-editor friend Myles Connolly, who thought the original characters were "non-sympathetic, non-interest-grabbing … Your girl. Don't let her be a brat because she's an heiress, but because she's bored with being an heiress … And the man … Make him a guy we all know and like. Maybe a tough, crusading reporter … And when he meets the spoiled heiress – well, it's *The Taming of the Shrew*" (quoted in Capra, 1971: 183). Ellie's transformation into a "brat" and into Shakespeare's tamed Kate is a twist on the far more balanced gender relations in Adams's short story. Peter repeatedly refers to Ellie as a "brat" in the film, while in the story the word appears only once, and it is Elspeth who uses it regretfully about herself, as Gottlieb (1988: 135) reminds us.

Along the same lines, the invocation of Shakespeare's ferocious but eventually submissive Kate suggests that the taming and educating in the film is one-way: Ellie is the child/shrew who needs to grow up, be subdued, and settle down, while Peter is the one who needs to discipline her, educate her, and do the taming. Likewise, turning the character of Peter into a reporter (as opposed to an inventor) drew on the cultural capital of the journalist figure. This figure had become popular in early 1930s cinema because of films such as *Gentlemen of the Press* (1929), *The Front Page* (1931), *Scandal Sheet* (1931), and *The Great Edition* (1932). According to film historian Thomas Doherty, the newspaperman was in the same category as the gangster, "another fast-talking, disreputable denizen of the urban underworld … hard-drinking and insubordinate" (1999: 187). So the original trajectory, at least as imagined by this trio of godfather writers, assumed male power and authority over the "brat," even though the resulting film offers far more complex gender relations (as described in chapter 1).

The stars who eventually signed up for *It Happened One Night* in November 1933 were by all accounts reluctant to take the roles. Clark Gable, a new sex symbol known primarily as a movie tough guy, was on loan from MGM. As studios were able to do in those days, Gable was lent to Columbia for *It Happened One Night* (for a salary of $10,000, interestingly, the sum of the reward being offered by Mr. Andrews in the film). Gable reported in 1936 that he was not very happy about the assignment because "the whole thing looked sour," and he resented being sent from MGM to a far less prestigious studio (Spicer, 2002: 103). Claudette Colbert found the script unappealing and was anxious to leave Los Angeles for a ski vacation in Idaho, but she was lured to the film by a salary of $50,000, despite her worry about its low-budget looks.

It Happened One Night was a quickie, which was typical for studio-produced films of the era. It was cast in November 1933, shot in 36 days, and previewed on January 28, 1934 in Pasadena, opening in New York City on February 23, 1934 (McBride, 1992: 308–9). Although critical reception in New York and Los Angeles was positive, openings in big cities across the country saw only modest ticket sales. The turnaround occurred in small towns, where theaters held it over week after week and continued repeat engagements for over a year. As Ed Sikov points out, the film made its money not in big-city movie palaces, but in "smaller, ordinary theaters … where audiences weren't surrounded by the trappings of luxury," and this is "where the film touched a nerve" (1989: 90). The conditions in this smaller market were ripe for the film in other ways. Maltby reports that small-town theater exhibitors had been protesting the gangster films and sophisticated comedies booked by the studios and were looking for "simple romances." As a result, the profits for *It Happened One Night* were the fifth largest of any film in 1934 (Maltby, 1998: 145, 162 n. 64).

In his autobiography, Capra paints the picture of small-town America saving a movie that sophisticated critics had dismissed – a Capraesque plot line: reviewers "were caught with their adjectives down" (1971: 159). In truth, the reviews were good and the adjectives hold up. Several reviews expressed surprise that the clichéd bus-trip formula had been turned into something entertaining and original. *Variety* (1934) praised the film's "intangible quality of charm" and the "deft direction of Frank Capra." The *New York Times* called it a "screen feast" bound to "generate plenty of laughter … blessed with bright dialogue" (Hall, 1934: 23). The *New York Herald Tribune* described it as "lively and amusing," with characters "played attractively by the two stars" (Watts, 1934: 14). The *New York Telegraph* admired the characters because they "behave like real human beings" (Boehnel, 1934). *The Nation* praised the film as having "exceptional movement, variety of every kind, and an ample infusion of tart commentary … one of the most uniformly amusing films of the season" (Troy, 1934: 314). Several reviews commented on the surprising simplicity of the story – perhaps in response to the complicated and sensationalistic bedroom comedies and women's films of the era (as described in chapter 3). *Vanity Fair*, which called the film "consistently entertaining," echoed a line of Clark Gable's: "Simple pleasures for simple people" (Norton, 1934: 50). Only the *New Yorker* gave the film a wholly negative review, and perhaps this is the one Capra remembers when he claims that "sophisticated" reviewers nixed it. "The picture is pretty much nonsense and quite dreary" in its treatment of "the mundane matter of travel by bus," the reviewer complained (Mosher, 1934: 59).

The success of *It Happened One Night* gave a considerable boost to Columbia Pictures, increasing its earnings over the previous year by nearly $270,000 and bringing in $1 million in its first run (McBride, 1992: 309). In Hollywood's 1930s production system, Columbia was a minor studio on the level of Universal Pictures, relatively small-time players next to MGM, Twentieth Century-Fox, Paramount, RKO, and Warner Brothers – the studios that owned their own theaters and had the most resources and capital. *It Happened One Night* spearheaded a cycle of romantic comedies for Columbia, securing its reputation as a niche for this genre – *Twentieth Century* (1934), *The Whole Town's Talking* (1935), *She Married Her Boss* (1935) – and then the ones that became classics – *The Awful Truth* (1937), *Holiday* (1938), and *Only Angels Have Wings* (1939) (Schatz, 1998: 24–5). However, *It Happened One Night* was not Columbia's overnight ticket to the big time, as has sometimes been reported in film lore. Columbia had expanded and increased its output of movies in the early 1930s in an effort to join the ranks of the major studios, so its gross revenues had already increased from $250,000 in 1926 to $11 million in 1933–4, reaching $20 million in 1937. As Brian Taves explains, this still did not put Columbia in the ranks of MGM, but *It Happened One Night* showed that "Columbia was more than a Poverty Row outfit, a studio of occasional possibilities" (1998: 228).

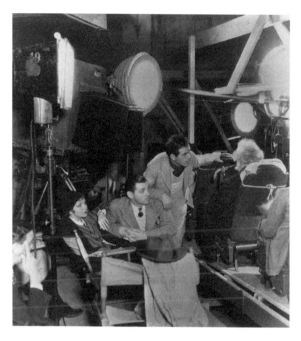

Claudette Colbert and Clark Gable with director Frank Capra on the set of *It Happened One Night*. Courtesy of Photofest.

Capra and Authorship

The impact of *It Happened One Night* on its director Frank Capra is, likewise, somewhat more complicated than traditional film histories imply. Capra eventually became best known for this comedy and some of the films he made subsequent to it, in particular *Mr. Smith Goes to Washington* (1939), *Meet John Doe* (1941), and *It's a Wonderful Life* (1946). Certainly the 1934 hit marked a career shift for the director, especially after the Academy Award sweep, so that in his autobiography he talks about it as "Winning the Grail" (1971: 159–89). In truth, though, in 1934 Capra was already the leading director at Columbia, a studio that had been promoting him as a celebrity filmmaker with a special appeal to women (Smoodin, 2004: 32–5). Overall, his most productive period was his previous era at Columbia (1929–33), and recent film scholarship has focused on the importance of these early years (Sklar, 1998: 37–8; Sklar & Zagarrio, 1998a: 2–4). So Capra did not suddenly emerge as a sought-after producer and household name but, after the financial success of *It Happened One Night*, he was rewarded with a higher salary, an unprecedented six-picture deal, and considerably more artistic freedom (Schatz, 1998: 23).

Capra also developed a reputation as a much-loved popular film-maker whose common-folk protagonists triumphed over those with power and money. This was an especially powerful narrative during the Depression. His warm portrayals of ordinary life and class soli-darity appealed to the huge number of Americans who had sustained enormous losses and were comforted by "the Capra touch" of comedy, social mobility, and optimism. His later films, which lionized the common citizen pitted against huge government forces, appealed to those who feared the centralized power of New Deal policies (Muscio, 1998: 181). In his study of the cultural reception and uses of Capra's films, Eric Smoodin (2004: 76–7, 87–94) notes that in the era's debates about morality in Hollywood movies, *It Happened One Night* was fre-quently invoked as an example of uplifting filmmaking. Capra's archives include letters from high school students who had been assigned to study the film for its moral significance and "lessons."

In his autobiography, Capra claims total credit for every film, defending his "simple notion of 'one man, one film'" which was for him "a fixation, an article of faith." Asserting that he "walked away" from any film he "could not control completely from conception to delivery," he argued that no great art "was ever created by committee" (1971: 34). Nevertheless, we now have extensive evidence of the studio "committee" work on his films, as well as documentation by McBride about the uncredited work done by writers and editing teams. *It Happened One Night* was a particularly sensitive topic for Capra, who began to give interviews about his contributions to Riskin's script even before the film was released (McBride, 1992: 292–8). Sources now agree that Capra was deeply involved in script revisions and that his collaborations with Riskin and others were highly productive. As a result, *It Happened One Night* illustrates the themes of class and everyday life that became Capra's hallmark, as well as his complicated attitudes toward Wasp power and privilege (as detailed in chapter 3). An Italian immigrant, Capra was known in Hollywood as "the Little Wop," so it is not surprising that an outsider's perspective inflects his work.

Beyond the teamwork with scripts, Capra's filmmaking at Columbia was also affected by specific conditions there. The Riskin–Capra scripts were successful because they were visualized by cinematographer Joe Walker, who supervised the camera work on all Capra's 1930s films, insuring a consistent look to these movies. In addition, although Columbia president Harry Cohn did not directly handle Capra's films, he controlled budgets and casting, and he delegated the supervision of Capra with regard to the details of sets and locations to associate producer Sam Briskin (Schatz, 1998: 22–3). The studio influenced the themes and ideology of Capra's films as well. Their pro-Roosevelt, New Deal ethos was aligned with the economic powers behind Columbia, which stood to profit from government constraints on the free market (Buscombe, 1998: 263–70). Further institutional directives were imposed by the 1930 censorship codes of the Motion Picture Producers and Distributors of America, which placed constraints on how topics of sexuality and gender could be represented.

In even broader terms, *It Happened One Night* emerged from the storytelling conventions that by 1934 had proven highly profitable in the Hollywood studio system. Romantic comedy, with its focus on the couple, was well suited to its conventions of style and editing, such as two-shot compositions (Haskell, [1974] 1987: 194). These conventions also included the gendered practices of voyeurism and fetishization of the female body, the privileging of spectacle, and the star system, which enabled identification of personalities from film to film.

The following chapters take these cinematic traditions and codes into account while analyzing the key contexts and themes of *It Happened One Night*. Chapter 1 focuses on the film as romantic comedy and as the site of critical debate about gender and marriage, examining in detail the scenes that introduce the main characters. Chapter 2 discusses sex and censorship, specifically how the film produced a version of "sexiness" within the constraints of the studio system and the 1930 Production Code, and how it provided a model for the treatment of sex when the Code was more strictly enforced from 1934 onwards. The two "walls of Jericho" motel scenes are analyzed in this chapter. Chapter 3 examines *It Happened One Night* within the context of the Depression, focusing on 1930s class and economic issues, especially in the auto-camp scene and the final sequence at the Andrews estate. This chapter also discusses the influence of Capra in the film's representation of class conflict. Finally, chapter 4 explores the star image and performances of Claudette Colbert and Clark Gable, who bring to the main characters specific personas and embodiments of gender ideals. The hitchhiking and wedding scenes get special attention in this chapter. Throughout, this book poses questions with the expectation that *It Happened One Night* will continue to provoke critical thinking about romance, marriage, and American ideas about class. Like its famous prop, a blanket that becomes the walls of Jericho, this film keeps transforming its meanings for generations of audiences and critics with varying ideas about what it reveals, what it covers up, and what it prompts us to imagine.

Chapter 1

Rules and Unruliness
Romantic Comedy

Gender and Genre

We love this movie. We've seen it in a hundred variations and know exactly how it ends. The couple often "meet cute" – airplane (or bus) seating, a stop to ask for directions, a bet made in a bar, a shared telephone party line – and this chance meeting later seems like fate. The woman may be a little crazy, and the guy has no idea how much he needs her. Their quarrels and at least one huge misunderstanding threaten to break them up. But in the last shot they're lip-locked, and we want to believe this is true love, happily ever after.

It Happened One Night has many literary and cinematic precedents, but it's usually considered the foundation of the romantic comedy film genre produced and refined in its classic period, the 1930s and early 1940s. Its imitations and reproductions show no sign of stopping. Following a lull in the 1970s, often attributed to gender anxieties in the wake of the women's movement, the genre picked up again in the 1980s.[1] This chapter focuses on *It Happened One Night* as romantic comedy and considers the critical debates about the film's take on romance, gender, and marriage. Film genres are categories identified by story, style, iconography, recurring stars, and formulas that get repeated – and remain box office draws – because they speak to cultural desires, anxieties, and fantasies. The romantic comedy film is one of our favorite stories about courtship, coupling, and falling in love. It's a sexy topic, and its sexiness yields box office returns but it is also yielding in its flexibility, responding to changing ideas about sexuality and gender. At first, these films had to end in marriage or the promise of marriage or remarriage, as in *Bringing Up Baby* (1938), *The Philadelphia Story* (1940), *Pillow Talk* (1959). But by the end of the twentieth century the genre included gay romantic comedies – *The Wedding Banquet* (1993), *But I'm a Cheerleader* (1999) – and soon acknowledged bisexuality and the instability of sexual orientation and desire: *Chasing Amy* (1997), *Kissing Jessica Stein* (2001), *Imagine Me and You* (2005), *Puccini for Beginners* (2006).

The template for all these stories – the obstacles, the romancing of exceptional characters, and the happy ending – is Shakespearean comedy (Evans & Deleyto, 1998: 2–5). *The Taming of the Shrew* was cited by Capra's editor friend during the script revision of *It Happened One Night* (as noted earlier). But the farcical tone and caricatures of that play do not actually match the more interesting tensions and characters of the Capra film or of Hollywood's best comic romances of the 1930s and 1940s. *It Happened One Night* actually shares the same narrative pattern of the more subtle Shakespearean comedy *As You Like It* – the young woman escaping from authority and traveling in disguise, meeting a lover in a place far removed from urban cynicism (Poague, 1977: 347).

However, the Shakespeare play most imitated in romantic comedy films is *Much Ado about Nothing*. Its bickering lovers Beatrice and Benedick are reborn in cinema's witty, fast-talking romantic couples of the 1930s, and the play was itself adapted into a film by Kenneth Branagh in 1993, at the height of the rejuvenation of this genre. Many romantic comedy films, including *It Happened One Night*, also share the incipient darkness of *Much Ado*, the underlying anxiety that men and women can't trust each other, that love may not be enough to fill the horrifying gap between the sexes. In *Much Ado*, an idyllic wedding scene is brutally disrupted with the groom's false charge that his bride is a whore. The falsely accused bride must undergo a symbolic death to be reborn again for the repentant groom in a second wedding. In *It Happened One Night*, the lovers are bitterly isolated from each other in the final third of the film, each certain the other has betrayed the relationship. As in *Much Ado*, a second wedding takes place which reverses the gloom and provides the happy ending, but not until each of the lovers has suffered some dark moments of the soul.

In both *It Happened One Night* and *Much Ado about Nothing*, the new couple symbolizes the beginning of a better society, the replacement of the aging father by the energetic young man who has claimed the daughter as bride. This pattern places romantic comedy, from Shakespeare through Capra, within the older and larger genre of New Comedy, the utopian narrative that celebrates social renewal through the newly formed couple, as described by Northrop Frye in his overview of literary genres (1957: 163). In the Capra film, the union of the middle-class working man Peter Warne and the heiress Ellen Andrews is an especially potent symbol of a utopian future, a leveling of class difference that must have spoken powerfully to Depression-era audiences.

New Comedy also emphasizes the formation of the couple rather than the usurpation of the father, so it "demands a place for women, or more precisely, for *a* woman, in the narrative itself," as Rowe points out (1995: 102). For Rowe, the romantic comedy film is the primary site in Hollywood cinema where the unruly woman, one of Western culture's most transgressive female figures, can thrive. The comedy structure, she argues, is also sympathetic to women because of its anti-authoritarian impulses and the mockery of macho posturing. In *It Happened One Night*, for example, Peter's swaggering hitchhiking demonstrations lead to the comic deflation of his cocky thumb. This film exemplifies the genre's playful gender reversals, too. In key scenes, Ellie is wearing Peter's clothes (coat, pajamas, bathrobe, scarf), and she takes the male prerogative in pushing aside the walls of Jericho to declare her love. Peter does the cooking, irons her clothes, and at one point poses in bed, "hands behind his head, elbows out, like an actress in a glamour pose" (Poague, 1994: 118). Comedy also provides a narrative where female desire – the desire that impels Ellie first to jump overboard and later to bolt from her own wedding – is not punished or regretted, as usually happens in melodrama (Rowe, 1995: 99–102, 112). As this chapter shows, many feminists have embraced romantic comedy, despite its larger conservative agenda of conformity to marriage. It's the film genre that foregrounds the problem of equality within a heterosexual relationship and emphasizes the woman's quest for that status. And it remains the preeminent female Hollywood genre. Female freedom and transgression are key components in the debates around romantic comedy and particularly around *It Happened One Night*, posing perplexing questions of what this unruly woman gains and loses in her story.

Romantic comedy and its spunky women thrived on stage for centuries after Shakespeare, from Restoration theater through the comedies of Oscar Wilde and George Bernard Shaw (DiBattista, 2001: 31). In cinema, the refinement of sound technology of the early 1930s – the "talkies" – enabled movies to deliver the crucial elements of witty conversation and sexually charged banter. The early romantic comedy films, often written by playwrights imported from the New York stage, imitated theatrical drawing-room comedy and focused on the upper classes, as seen in the elegant Ernst Lubitsch comedies and in classics such as *Dinner at Eight* (1933). *It Happened One Night*, with its inclusion of an unemployed reporter and its move out of the yacht and onto the Greyhound bus, broke away from that pattern and inaugurated the conventions now standard in the genre: identifiable characters, everyday settings, and social obstacles – culture, class, politics, race, nationality, or background – that make the romance unlikely. Inevitably, these social conflicts are subsumed by the sexual and romantic ones. The reporter marries the heiress, but the rhetoric of the film convinces us it's really about sex, not class. Or as Rowe puts it, this genre uses "romantic love to absorb all other needs, desires, and contradictions, to promise the fulfillment not only of sexual desire but of *all* desire" (1995: 129). As a result, the desire most quickly absorbed and repressed is the heroine's drive for autonomy and independence.

In this way, romantic comedy as modeled in *It Happened One Night* pits the unruliness of its characters against the rules of the genre and, in a larger sense, the social rules. No matter how wildly unconventional these individuals may be, they will move toward the conventional marriage. Peter and Ellie are goofy enough to ask for a toy trumpet for their honeymoon, but before we see the walls of Jericho blanket drop in the final shot, we hear the auto-camp proprietors tell us they've seen the marriage certificate. Neither the trumpet nor the certificate actually appears on screen, but these are the props of the genre, symbols of playfulness and legitimacy.

Surveying critical perspectives on film genres, Rick Altman points out two schools of thought. One theory of film genres sees them as social "rituals" with the community goal of validating our cultural practices (i.e., heterosexuality, marriage, monogamy) and resolving their contradictions (individualism, the randomness of desire). Understood this way, romantic comedy celebrates both the American-style rugged individual but also marriage – with all its compromises – as the place for the stubborn individualist: Peter Warne, the reporter who writes in free verse, and Ellie Andrews, the rich daughter who dives from the yacht in her dressing gown. The other stand on film genres is that they do the ideological work of maintaining the status quo. Gay and bisexual romantic comedies may appear as alternatives, but the overwhelming majority of these films tell us to be heterosexual and to marry. Likewise, romantic comedy idealizes monogamy and long-term commitment, but not the qualities that actually sustain them – loyalty, endurance, patience, friendship. Instead, it primes the pump of excitement that begins every relationship but cannot possibly last. The closing shot is the embrace or kiss, not the future colicky babies, aging bodies, and mounting debts. While the "ritual" theorists see genres "offering *imaginative* solutions to a society's real problems," the ideology theorists see genres "luring audiences into accepting *deceptive* non-solutions" (Altman, 1999: 27). These gender–genre tensions shape many of the arguments around *It Happened One Night*, particularly around the question of what the film suggests about marriage and about its rebellious heroine.

Screwball Characters Meet Cute

Hollywood's romantic comedies of the 1930s and 1940s have been designated "screwball" comedies, a term that emerged from the 1920s slang word "screwy" to describe insanity. When Mr. Andrews asks Peter outright if he loves Ellie, Peter shouts, "Yes, but don't hold that against me. I'm a little screwy myself!" *It Happened One Night* is often considered the first screwball comedy, even if it lacks the frantic physical antics of some of the later ones.[2] In the 1930s, "screwball" was a baseball term to describe a deliberately wild pitch designed to confuse the batter. Screwball comedy most often refers to a film featuring a madcap hero and heroine and their unpredictable behavior, but it also denotes "a sense of confusion about romance and human relations" (Sikov, 1989: 19). In *It Happened One Night*, the opening sequences introducing Peter and Ellen illustrate the key qualities of both screwball comedy and the wider genre of the romantic comedy film: the brash characters, the "meet cute," the seeds of conflict, and the sense of confusion about love and relationships.[3] These two sequences also reveal a hero and heroine who are thoroughly different in significant ways – in social class and background – and alarmingly similar in volatile ways – equally reckless and fiercely resistant to authority.

The film's establishing shot shows a sleek luxury yacht, followed by a medium shot of Mr. Andrews and the chief steward dressed in nautical uniforms of dark jacket, white trousers, and cap. The casting of stout Walter Connolly as Mr. Andrews and the military-style costume instantly characterize him as someone who throws his weight around and is accustomed to being obeyed, if not saluted. This *mise en scène* also establishes the overall structure of male clout; this ship and family are run by men in uniforms. The curt exchange about the daughter's refusal of food and the bullying command to "jam it down her throat" set up the gender and generational conflicts before the daughter even appears.

In fact, we hear her before we see her. The first scene ends with a shot of Mr. Andrews' portly figure striding purposefully toward the camera, on his way to Ellie's cabin. In the next shot, the crew hovers at the closed cabin door to eavesdrop on the conversation, and we too overhear her obstinate proclamation: "I'm not going to eat a thing until you let me off this boat." Maria DiBattista has characterized the romantic comedy film heroine of the 1930s and 1940s as, most of all, the woman who talks back, the fast-talking dame. Her power of speech, her sassiness, her argumentative voice, DiBattista claims, "paved a way for a new class or sort of woman who finally would answer to no one but herself" (2001: 11). Significantly, Ellie's first line in this romantic comedy is the declaration of her autonomy over her own body. Historically, the hunger strike draws on the one power, the choice to eat or starve, that even the powerless retain. The use of this politically charged tactic on a luxury yacht is not without irony, but it makes the point about the power structure in this family. The fact that the strike is protesting the father's interference in an unconsummated marriage amplifies the theme of bodies and the conflict of desires.

When we first see her, Ellie is facing away from the camera, her father behind her with his hands on her shoulders. In sharp contrast to his earlier bullying rant, Mr. Andrews is using a wheedling, coaxing tone we sense he has used before, telling her she knows he'll eventually have his way. She quickly shrugs out of his embrace. "This time you won't," she assures him coldly and stalks across the room to make a speech about how she and King Westley are already legally married. In contrast to Mr. Andrews' dark military-style jacket, Ellie is wearing a white satin dressing gown, suggesting femininity and vulnerability, but buttoned chastely high at the neck. The sexiness is in her voice. Ellie makes her clincher argument about her elopement – "I'm over 21 and so is he" – in "a pouting, honeyed voice," says Kendall, that turns it "into a slightly risqué song" (1990: 40). Ellie is also smoking a cigarette, which in 1934 was still cutting-edge behavior for women and associated with female independence.[4]

As Ellie's anger escalates from frustration to fury, the shot compositions emphasize the terms of the duel: Mr. Andrews' dark, bulky figure contrasted with Ellie's light, slim one. She does most of the moving in this scene – pacing, practically bouncing against the walls – and her lightness and mobility will prove to be her advantage. Exasperated with her father's interference, she turns to face the camera so we can see emotion animate her face as she takes a drag of her cigarette and, with contempt, exhales the smoke at Mr. Andrews, who threatens that she and Westley will "never live under the same roof." By the time the steward arrives with trays of food, Ellie's voice and posture are simmering with rage, and he is cowering in fear at her rebuke.

The meal is Mr. Andrews' ploy to make Ellie hungry by eating in front of her. "So subtle," she says sarcastically, rolling her eyes. Here we learn of Mr. Andrews' other heavy-handed tactics in sending his "gorillas," as Ellie puts it, to drag her away from the justice of the peace just

Ellie reacts with cold fury when her father has a tray of food delivered to break her hunger strike. Courtesy of Photofest.

after the wedding ceremony. He does this kind of thing, he tells her, because she's "a stubborn idiot," provoking her reply that she "comes from a long line of stubborn idiots," all of this information being crucial in the larger power dynamics of daughter, father, and lover in the film. The other important plot information imparted during their argument is that Ellie may have married Westley purely to spite her father, who loathes Westley as "a fake." So the question of her desire is immediately complicated. Does she want this man and marriage or does she simply want whatever her father opposes? Is this the story of Ellie learning what she really desires – something a man needs to teach her – or the story of female rebellion against paternal authority? The narrative goes both ways, but the question is whether we read romantic comedy as empowering for women or as a more conservative story about women learning to want the right man.

Continuing to treat her as a child who can be swayed with a bribe, Mr. Andrews makes the mistake of pushing the food toward her just as Ellie is proclaiming that she will shout if she wants to, and in fact scream if she wants to. It has a boomerang effect. His paternal behavior provokes her inner brat. When he waves a forkful of "nice, juicy steak" in her face, the camera catches a close-up of Ellie, now seething with fury, a little smile at the corner of her mouth to indicate how much she is enjoying her tantrum. She slaps away the fork and then upsets the entire food tray. In a rapid shot/countershot, Mr. Andrews slaps her across the face, and we see first her shock and then his own shock and regret. The implication is that this physical violence has never happened before and has created a serious breach in the relationship of two "stubborn idiots" who nevertheless love each other.

A hallmark of the screwball comedy is physical action – clowning tumbles, car chases, the race to a departing train or plane. The slap galvanizes Ellie into action. She bolts out the door, pushing aside the eavesdropping stewards, and begins her climb over the rail of the yacht. A shot of Mr. Andrews running toward the camera is followed by a quick shot of Ellie pausing just for a moment on the rail, narrowing her eyes at her father in triumphant revenge. The next shot is her athletic dive into the water, unimpeded by the long dressing gown, a glorious gesture of quickness, youth, and spontaneity that the portly Mr. Andrews, encumbered in his uniform, cannot possibly match. In an intriguing detail, Mr. Andrews then gives an order to telephone the detective agency that "Ellen Andrews has escaped again." Again? Was the first escape the elopement, or is there a longer history of escapes from and retrievals by Daddy? The entire yacht sequence takes less than three minutes, wittily and economically summing up the romantic heroine as an argumentative young woman, headstrong enough to jump into a bay in her dressing gown, who has "escaped" at least once before.

The following sequence, the "meet cute," links Ellie to Peter through repeated shots and narrative details. A wipe – the scene or sequence transition Capra uses most often in this film – takes us to Ellie at a Greyhound bus station (filmed, like the other bus station scenes, at the Greyhound station in Los Angeles). We learn later that she's

The "meet cute" places Ellie and Peter within the narrow confines of a shared seat on an overnight bus. Courtesy of Photofest.

pawned her jewelry for money to buy traveling clothes, and she's talked a grandmotherly woman into purchasing a bus ticket for her so she can avoid her father's detectives. In short, despite the impulsive dive, Ellie has proven herself an adept and clever fugitive. Nevertheless, this character later becomes helpless and impractical once she starts traveling with Peter.

The sequence in which they meet begins with a tracking shot connecting the two main characters through other Greyhound passengers, prefiguring the film's use of bus riders and working-class travelers as the everyday context for the unfolding romance. The shot follows Ellie's gaze to the old woman walking across the lobby to deliver the ticket. Ticket in hand, Ellie walks offscreen left while the camera tracks in the opposite direction, following an anonymous male passenger across the lobby to a rowdy crowd of men in front of a telephone booth. In drunken voices, the men tell him history is being made, and in a subtle comic touch, they push him offscreen so they can better lean in to hear one side of the phone conversation. The shot composition parallels the earlier one of the yacht crew leaning toward the cabin door to hear the argument between Ellie and her father. As a result, long before the two main characters actually meet, they have been visually and dramatically linked as people whose arguments draw an audience.

We are introduced to Peter Warne in a tight close-up inside the booth, looking far more like a gangster than a lover. His face is wedged to the right of the frame and three-quarters encased in shadow, the raucous crowd of men slightly out of focus behind him. Given Clark Gable's previous film persona, the 1930s audience would have expected another tough gangster from him. But the effect is comedy, not menace, because his voice is slurred and his hat sits too far back on his head. Also, unlike Ellie's passionate argument with her father about marriage and autonomy, this argument is about words, language, and writing style. It's both more pompous and a great deal sillier. Peter drunkenly calls his editor a "monkey face" and a "gas house palooka" for not recognizing him as a good newspaper reporter and not appreciating the story he wrote "in free verse." Peter's childish name-calling positions him as the bratty child who is old enough to drink too much and who likes to show off to a crowd. Like Ellie, he represents the younger generation making a grand romantic gesture that the older generation doesn't understand – not a secret marriage but newspaper stories written in an imaginative poetic style.

During the argument, the reverse shots reveal Joe, the editor, as a father figure much like Mr. Andrews, middle-aged, portly, and laden with the props of authority – in this case, desk, papers, telephones, cigar. After their brief, angry exchange, he fires Peter, telling him he wouldn't know a good newspaper story if it "kicked [him] in the pants," and hangs up in disgust. But Peter pretends the argument is still going on and that Joe is begging him to stay on the job. This is the first of several moments of improvisation and self-conscious play-acting for others seen in this film.

A much more serious issue lies just beneath the humor of the name-calling and the quarrel about writing style. Peter is a man who has just lost his job. When Joe cuts short the argument by angrily telling him that he is absolutely finished at the newspaper, the close-up shows Peter taken aback. Shaken, he loses his aplomb for a moment before recovering his pluck and pretending that Joe is still on the phone begging him to come back. The tipsy eavesdropper's comment, "This is history in the making," reminds us of a grim history. The 1934 audience had seen almost five years of lost jobs and low employment. A man talking back to his boss, calling him names, taunting his authority, refusing to go back to the job, is a great deal bolder than Ellie's dive into the bay. Ellie can always change her mind, get off the bus, and resume a pampered life. As Thomas Schatz puts it, Ellie is "simply swimming from one yacht to another," whereas Peter is on the road with a few bucks in his pocket and no paycheck in sight (1981: 153).

Though Peter has lost more, this brief introductory scene suggests that he and Ellie are equals in their need for direction and prudence. After all, does Peter want a job as a poet or a reporter? In a comical reversal of meanings, this scene also links them by identifying Peter as the other "king" in the narrative, as he is hailed by his drunken friends outside the phone booth. Up to this point, we have seen him only in shadowy noir-style close-ups, but the first medium shot of Peter is humbly demystifying. Surrounded by men in suit jackets, Peter alone wears a natty scarf and a baggy, wrinkled topcoat, which will become an important prop later in the story. Overall, Peter is one shade seedier than his companions, and his shabby attire contributes to the comic effect of his assumption of haughty stateliness. Straightening his back and pulling himself up, Peter lifts his chin with the dignity of royalty, wraps his coat and scarf around himself like an ermine cape, and asks if his "chariot" is ready, his face carefully composed with the gravity of a sovereign who has just made a sad but wise decision. This is the topsy-turvy world of carnival – the unemployed drunk crowned king – building up to the meeting with the other character in reversed circumstances, the rich young woman disguised as a traveler on the Greyhound bus. This is also the performance of an unemployed man with great imagination, instantly transforming himself into royalty, preening himself with an inward eye despite the external scruffiness.

Peter's meeting with Ellie involves one more encounter with authority, a comic one that reinforces their equal arrogance. On the crowded bus, Peter discovers that the only unoccupied seat is piled with bundled newspapers. His question about this to the scowling bus driver is polite enough, but when he gets no reply he shows no hesitation in throwing the bundles out of the bus window to the sidewalk below, a simple but gutsy gesture of the little guy versus the system, symbolically replaying the fight with the editor. His ensuing squabble with the driver is light in tone, but the inarticulate driver is no match for witty Peter, who claims victory by drawing approving laughter from the crowd on the bus – again, a show-off performance for an audience.

The initial intersection of Peter and Ellie is set up as a visual joke. A medium shot shows Peter and the bus driver in their dispute, which has developed into Peter's tall tale about what happened once when he sat on a newspaper and the front page got imprinted on the seat of his pants. Neither of them pays attention when Ellie enters the shot and crosses in front of them, pushing against the driver and edging past Peter, heading for what the audience knows is the last remaining seat on the bus, the topic of the ongoing squabble. When Peter realizes what has happened – the seat for which he fought has been appropriated by a stranger – he utters the quaintly phrased line which is famous as one of screwball's most clever double entendres: "Excuse me, lady, but that upon which you sit is mine."

Peter has just told a comic story about his own backside being read like a newspaper, but the oblique reference to Ellie's backside is sexual as well as comic, positioning Peter as the aggressive claimant of Ellie's body. Ellie's cool response, a question to the driver confirming that the seats are not reserved, is to claim her space. But Peter then asks the driver if it's a double seat, not a single one, invoking romantic comedy's iconic doubleness (two singles becoming a pair) as well as double sexual meaning. Peter wedges himself in next to Ellie, the first of many small spaces they will share with more or less comfort. The scene ends with one more visual joke about seats, backsides, and physical space. Doggedly ignoring Peter's offer to stow her bag on the top rack,

Ellie chooses to stand up and hoist up her bag at the moment the bus lurches forward. Caught off balance, she lurches onto Peter's lap, giving him not only sudden intimacy with her backside but also the opportunity to have the last word: "Next time you drop in, bring your folks."[5] As she settles in beside him, a medium two-shot lingers on their faces, his relaxed and smug, hers at first prim and taut but slowly breaking into a small smile. So both the dialogue and the visual comedy of the meeting scene shrewdly set up the issues that shape the narrative: the reluctant sharing of space, sexual tension, the development of intimacy, and Ellie's "folks" hovering in the background.

Intimacy, Violence, and Marriage

In addition to introducing these key themes, this first bus scene contains a trite line of dialogue with implications that ripple throughout the narrative and signal the film's larger concerns with gender and romance. During Peter's argument with the bus driver, the driver makes a cranky threat: "What you need's a good sock on the nose." This launches Peter into a theatrical riff about how much he likes his nose the way it is. But the larger point is that Peter himself uses a variation of this line at the end of the film when Mr. Andrews asks him if he loves Ellie. Peter's reply is oddly elliptical: "What she needs is a guy that will take a sock at her once a day whether it's coming to her or not." These rhetorical threats bookending the narrative serve as ironic commentaries on what these characters "need" – ironic because the rhetoric of romantic comedy suggests that what they really need, of course, is each other. However, the overtones of the threats and the question of "need" are at once more complex and more disturbing than that.

The concept of "need" is complicated throughout the film, beginning with Ellie's rich-girl hunger strike, in which food is a bargaining chip for someone who has never actually been hungry. As the road trip goes on, Ellie meets some truly needy people – the woman who faints from hunger and the little boy who says they haven't eaten anything for a day. Shortly thereafter, when their money is gone, Ellie and

Peter are themselves genuinely hungry. Even then, Ellie refuses the "horrid" raw carrots Peter finds for her. Stanley Cavell points out that this refusal of the carrots indicates her spoiled "sense of exemption from the human condition" (1981: 93). Her refusal of food, first from her father and then from Peter, is also a refusal of love, so that when she finally does eat the raw carrots, it signals not only her acceptance of Peter's love, but "her acceptance of her humanity, of true need." Peter's neediness is more sketchily developed. Gruff and self-sufficient, at first he seems to need only a job and thus Ellie as the scoop that will get him back on the newspaper. But on the third night of the journey, he uses the hunger metaphor in his wishful soliloquy about his dreams of authenticity and spontaneity, saying, "Boy, if I could ever find a girl who's hungry for those things …," triggering a turning point of the story (Cavell 1981: 91–5).

So the wisecracks about needing "a sock" mock the structure of romantic comedy but also touch on these more serious questions about what exactly we need in order to be human. The threats of physical violence also hint at a darker machismo which haunts *It Happened One Night* and undermines its reading as liberating for women. The film opens with Mr. Andrews' brutish rant about jamming food down Ellie's throat. The rant is a bluff because, in the next scene, his tone with her is cajoling, not threatening. Nevertheless, he does use physical violence by the end of the scene. In fact, the prompt for all the narrative action is his slap of her face. The second "sock" in the film, far more playful, is Peter's slap of Ellie's behind as he carries her across the stream in the second half of the film, so the trajectory is a move from punishment to erotic play. Yet Peter's man-to-man talk with Mr. Andrews at the end of the film suggests a pact about controlling willful women. Physical force – "a sock at her once a day" – could encompass the coercive as well as the erotic. The overall suggestion is that women need – and/or want – to be hit.

In contrast, Peter needing "a sock," as threatened by the bus driver, has a very different effect, not only in relation to gender but by way of Gable's iconic status as a tough guy. Tough guys in movies always "need" to be hit so they can hit back more forcefully, proving their masculinity. The blustering conversation with the bus driver, even while it is comic, reinforces the film's narrative world as structured by male power, physical and social. For Maltby, Peter is desirable to both Ellie and her father because he understands "the necessary use of violence in the operation of patriarchal authority" (1998: 152).

The underlying violence is a genre issue too. Screwball comedies are known for their emphasis on "fast-flung insults and violence, either threatened or carried out" to signal the struggles of an equitable relationship (McDonald, 2007: 20). Ed Sikov's theory is that the "madcap" elements of screwball allow for the expression of hostilities otherwise suppressed in representations of romance. He argues that the violence is a release of sexual anxiety and "irrefutable evidence of intimacy," given how much tension is repressed in the "happy home," and points out that in this regard women "get a raw deal throughout the genre": they are the ones whose independence is physically punished by "resentful heroes" (Sikov, 1989: 28–9). Diane Carson claims that the physical abuse of women in these films has the effect of countering and silencing the fast-talking dame. The blows, bumps, and slaps, playful or otherwise, "disrupt and usurp the power of her voice. The message is clear: stay in your place" (1994: 216).

Yet, like other feminist readers of romantic comedy, Carson nonetheless emphasizes the female-empowering pleasures of these films. She finds the heroines' subversive energy a significant disruption of the status quo, despite the conventional narrative endings (1994: 223–4). Rowe, whose "unruly woman" argument develops this claim, maintains that in *It Happened One Night*, Ellie draws from the specific power of the virgin, the woman whose strength lies in her position outside of marriage, as reflected by the mythical figures of Athena, Artemis, and warrior Amazons. The hymen can be considered "a barrier that preserves a kind of independence in the romantic heroine." Ellie's power is her liminal position: she is married but still a virgin; she has escaped from her father but is not yet in the household of another man, neither child nor wife. She uses this position to *extend* the narrative, first by delaying her arrival in New York, and then by delaying the consummation of her marriage to Westley by demanding a formal wedding (Rowe, 1995: 133–5). Reinforcing this reading of the film, Kendall points out that it is

Two thumbs up or down? Critics are divided as to whether the road adventures of Peter and Ellie develop into a relationship of equals. Courtesy of Photofest.

"the woman who controls the action. She is the one who had set the plot in motion at the beginning and the one who saves the romance at the end" (1990: 49).

The argument against this reading – the interpretation of *It Happened One Night* as an essentially conservative, even reactionary, film in terms of its gender politics – emphasizes not only the latent violence but also the moments when Ellie is punished when she asserts herself. After all, even after she transgresses the walls of Jericho, the shocked Peter simply sends her back to her bed to cry. Maltby (1998) points out other instances: when she leaves Peter's seat on the bus, she is besieged by the sleazy salesman Shapeley, and when she argues with Peter the first night at the auto camp, he wins the argument by taking off his shirt, an overt sexual threat. Even more troubling is the extent to which Ellie is infantilized by Peter, and eventually takes pleasure in submitting to him like a child. He makes the rules about how to dunk a doughnut, how to spend money, and how to ride piggyback. By the time they spend the night in the hayfield, he "has reduced Ellie to a condition of complete childish dependence," wailing when she thinks she is abandoned, crying first for food and then for comfort. Maltby reads the film as "an exercise in the expression of control over Ellie's sexuality" by the father and then by the suitable husband. Peter reveals that he knows how to deal with money, expecting no more or less than his $36.90, and is thus "a suitable recipient for the other form of property, Ellie" (Maltby, 1998: 151–5).

Ellie's status – as unruly woman, as child, as property, as desiring heroine, as powerful virgin – is central to the film's larger theme of marriage. It is not simply that some readers want to claim Ellie as a heroine and others want to expose the film as patriarchal and sexist. Instead, the fascination and significance of *It Happened One Night* lies in its cultural work of figuring out what marriage entails. Many film scholars agree that romantic comedies emerged in the 1930s as a response to the decline of marriage and the spiking of divorce rates in the previous 10 years. This occurred as more women began to have choices about making a living and as the Victorian paradigm of domestic womanhood gave way to the liberated New Woman or flapper of the 1920s (as will be discussed in chapter 2). In response, a new "companionate" model of marriage emerged in the 1920s, promulgated in advice books and popular fiction, promoting equality, companionship, and romance as marital ideals. Screwball comedies showcased this modern egalitarian marriage, which in turn required an independent heroine who, by implication, was the cause of the new mode of relationship (Shumway, 2003: 67–9). The romantic comedy heroine, though not as overtly sexy as the flapper, shared her pluck, vivacious sense of fun, and willingness to treat men as partners and pals (Lent, 1995: 316–20).

Cavell, reading *It Happened One Night* as a film about marriage and the human condition, begins with this premise, too, arguing that the post-suffragist generation of women began to incorporate feminist ideas into personal issues of autonomy. He sees *It Happened One Night* as part of a cycle of films struggling with "the reciprocity or equality of consciousness between a woman and a man" (1981: 17). Far from seeing Ellie as a feminist heroine, however, Cavell characterizes her as a woman in need of an education and a teacher, a man who will show her how to acknowledge her own desire and how to become an autonomous person. She needs to be "created." Cavell claims that when Peter teaches Ellie the right way to dunk a doughnut, her reply, "Thanks, professor," acknowledges this teacher–student, creator–creature relationship (1981: 84).

However, Sikov, writing about the same scene, argues that Peter's lecture about dunking is an "irritating" revelation of his insecurities: "He's threatened by this attractive woman," and "Ellie isn't the kind of woman who will put up with too many of Peter's lessons" (1989: 88–90). Certainly Peter himself has a great deal to learn. As Rowe points out, Peter is blinded by his stubbornness about class boundaries and his alienation from his own emotional life. As a result, on the third night of the journey, he rhapsodizes about his island dream scenario without realizing it is exactly what he had experienced the night before, under the stars with Ellie. Rowe's interpretation is that only Ellie, with her virginal power, can transform and "create" the new Peter (1995: 131–2).

What both characters most need to learn is the meaning of marriage itself, in that the narrative offers two sham marriages – the one with Westley and the fictional one that Peter and Ellie maintain during their travels – before the "true" marriage that ends the film. But at what point in Peter and Ellie's journey do they move into the intimacy of a marriage? Cavell reminds us of the quarrel between Mr. Andrews and Ellie about her marriage to King Westley. Her primary argument is that she and Westley are "legally, actually married." Mr. Andrews' retort is that she's "never going to live under the same roof with him." It's a euphemism for the consummation of the marriage, but it raises the interesting question of what being "actually married" entails, because Ellie and Peter begin to "live under the same roof" on the first night of their journey. For Cavell, their relationship develops so that by the third night they indeed act like a married couple quietly preparing for bed, undressing and even putting up the blanket wall as a matter-of-fact domestic detail (1981: 84–6).

Further complicating the question of "real" marriage and intimacy is the meaning of their charade as a quarreling couple for the detectives in the first auto-camp sequence. When Mr. Andrews' detectives appear at the door of the cabin, Ellie wants to jump out the window, but Peter quickly decides that their best escape is to impersonate a married couple. This is significant because Ellie's previous escape jump, from the yacht, had been successful, but now she and Peter must act together as a couple to escape authority. The shot composition reinforces this. The divider blanket, acting as the walls of Jericho the previous night, had isolated Peter and Ellie into separate spaces in the frame. But now the hanging blanket divides the space between the couple on the left and the detectives on the right. The detectives and the auto-park owner are also now the audience, paralleling the eavesdroppers for whom Ellie and Peter had individually "made a scene" in the opening sequences. Now they make a scene together and, as Cavell points out, Peter immediately steps into the role of director, rearranging Ellie's hair and unbuttoning her top buttons (1981: 107). He himself unbuttons his vest and trousers to give the impression of domestic intimacy, a couple getting dressed together and gossiping about Aunt Bella.

The charade is a psychodrama, too, as Gottlieb suggests, with Peter ranting over Ellie's likeness to her stupid father and venting jealousy over a "big Swede" who is an obvious stand-in for King Westley. Ellie in turn gets an opportunity to scream at Peter and to cry about how badly he is treating her (Gottlieb, 1988: 133). Cavell believes they fool the detectives because the proof that they are a married couple is their squabbling, which for him suggests that "a willingness for marriage entails a certain willingness for bickering," a precept central to romantic comedy (1981: 86). The critic Ray Carney likewise links the charade scene to the issue of intimacy, claiming that an argument is "a close second to making love for the depth of involvement and emotional self-exposure it demands" (1996: 239). More troubling is that this charade of a quarrel implies physical violence as well. When Ellie wails at Peter's yelling, he raises his hand as if to strike her, a gesture that complements his threat to "take a sock" at the detectives for intruding into their privacy and approaching his wife. This fits the well-documented profile of the abusive spouse; the man who is willing to beat up someone to protect his woman is likely to beat up the woman as well.

This psychodrama also performs class. Ellie and Peter take on a catalog of stereotyped behavior. Both talk loudly: Ellie speaks in a broad Southern accent; Peter refers to family in Wilkes-Barre (a small town in Pennsylvania), and a dance at the Elks where, Ellie adds, he was drunk. But their charade exceeds the clichés. In the previous scene, Ellie had explained to Peter that being wealthy was no fun and that she'd "trade places with a plumber's daughter any day." In the faux quarrel, Peter uses her own words to belittle her: "Once a plumber's daughter, always a plumber's daughter." The accusation reverses their class standing. This working-class husband, whatever he does, is at least not as low in status as a plumber.

The class drama is also a sexual and material one in that the domain of plumbers is the lower body, culturally coded as the sphere of pleasure, dirt, looseness, and transgression (Bakhtin, 1984: 309–28). So their lower status is also a sexual status. This is further suggested by Peter's rearrangement of Ellie's clothes and body. He gives her a lower neckline and – not once, but three times – pushes apart her legs under her skirt to make sure she sits with her legs open – something "a lady" would never do, not even under a skirt, even though there is no frontal shot revealing the effect. The quarrel itself is about sex and gender expectation – his temper, her "butting in" to arguments, his protectiveness and jealousy, which are not at all repressed (as they are in "higher" culture) but are topics for a screaming argument. Following Carney's (1996) logic about the argument as intimate behavior, we can see how intimacy is coded as class, with sex located not in the luxury yachts of the Andrewses, but in the gritty world of couples at the auto camp.

The charade is also fun. Cavell emphasizes the importance of play for Ellie and Peter, "the pleasure of their own company," in the development of the relationship of marriage in this film (1981: 88). The performance for the detectives is the first occasion for Ellie and Peter to laugh together, giddy with the success of their little theatrical scene, which Peter wants to take to small-town auditoriums with the title "The Great Deception." Ellie wants to call it "Cinderella," or "A Hot Love Story," titles which Peter finds "too mushy." This conversation ensues as Peter kneels before her and rebuttons her blouse, an intimate gesture during which, for the first time, we see the sparks of attraction in their locked eyes. Their different titles for the charade show that Ellie, sooner than Peter, is willing to acknowledge an erotic or romantic element in their relationship. "She recognizes the nature of their relationship before he does," as Rowe points out (1995: 132). Even with their different interpretations of the play-acting, their ability to work and play together turns them into the kind of couple idealized by the romantic comedy – in this case, two people equally capable of improvisation and the bamboozling of authority.[6]

But is this what marriage is about? David Shumway takes the position that the relationship that develops between Peter and Ellie is far more like adultery than marriage. Though the early screwball comedies are often cited as representations of the modern, egalitarian marriage, Shumway argues that these films never show the marriage itself, focusing instead on escapades that pull the lovers away from ordinary, everyday life. For Shumway, the structure that is most important in *It Happened One Night* is the adulterous triad made up of Ellie, her husband King Westley, and Peter: the "adventure" of the film is essentially the adventure of adultery, even if they are technically chaste. Shumway's larger point is that the screwball comedy "mystifies" marriage by locating it offscreen, as the desire of the narrative but magically outside of it. Its "illusion," he argues, "is that one can have both complete desire and complete satisfaction and that the name for this state of affairs is marriage" (Shumway, 2003: 88–95). If these films tell us anything about marriage, they tell us that it's a patriarchal institution in which daughters are objects of exchange – father to husband – and in which "married women must become little girls," as is seen in Ellie's need for protection and her status as "brat" (97).

While Shumway characterizes *It Happened One Night* as an "illusion" about marriage and Maltby sees it as an exercise in patriarchal control, critics such as Rowe (1995) and Kendall (1990) characterize it as a fantasy about women making the dive or escape that allows them to reimagine their lives. In a genre characterized as "the battle of the sexes," this film inevitably participates in the gendered rereading of culture that has been influenced by feminist scholarship. Leland Poague argues that Capra himself needs to be reconsidered in this light, given a pattern of female identification in his films, an inclination to assign authorial values and perspective to women characters. Capra's films, he claims, show a protofeminist "interest in the human female as embodying the human as such" (Poague, 1994: 232). Again, the question often comes back to how we read Ellie, which is perhaps the question of who is doing the reading and how we identify our own desires as spectators.

The debate about gender and romance in *It Happened One Night* also participates in the wider culture of romance, which constantly promises "complete desire and complete satisfaction" in its portrayal of attractive, vivacious couples. They appear in advertisements for liquor and clothing, in celebrity culture, in reality dating shows, and in wedding magazines – all celebrating the extraordinary excitement of romance and glossing over the ordinary habits, duties, aches, and routines of long-term commitment.

Yet there is a moment in *It Happened One Night* when the ordinary, rather than the extraordinary, triumphs as a moment of intimacy. One of the most famous shots in the film, the one reproduced in the 1934 advertisements, is the moonlit close-up during the night in the hayfield, when Peter leans down to Ellie and they nearly kiss, both of them backlit, their profiles in soft focus. The next scene shows them on the road again, Ellie limping in her high heels and guiding them to pause for rest on a fence. This introduces the widely cited hitchhiking episode, in which Peter's arrogance is comically deflated by Ellie's use of her attractive legs to stop a car. However, the opening exchange in this scene is also remarkable. Wholly unselfconscious, Ellie whisks her finger around her front teeth and asks Peter for a toothpick because she has a piece of hay stuck in her teeth, which she exhibits to him by baring her gums as if she were at the dentist. Similarly unselfconscious, Peter pulls out a penknife, and a close-up shot shows them together, Peter holding the top of her head to keep her still, Ellie grimacing with her mouth wide open while he digs between her front teeth. The shot is nearly a graphic match for the moonlit shot in the previous scene, when Peter had likewise leaned toward her face. The clever link between the two shots is the hay, which on the previous night was material for a mattress and now is material for impromptu dentistry. Here, without moonlight, backlight, or flattering profiles, Peter similarly leans in from screen left, this time not to consider a kiss but to pick her teeth. This is the everyday intimacy of marriage, not always pretty to look at, attentive to ordinary needs, prone to the bodily mishaps that lend themselves to comedy.

Chapter 2

Sex and Censorship
The Wavering Walls of Jericho

The Hays Office and the Production Code

What exactly happened and on which night? The title of *It Happened One Night* might refer to the first night Peter and Ellie are together at the motel, separated by the fragile walls of Jericho. But "it" could also be the moment Peter bends down to her in the hayfield the following night, when their lips nearly touch and they are obviously drawn to each other. Perhaps "it" is Ellie's scandalous transgression of the blanket wall when they make their final stop at a motel before New York. And of course, "it" could be the wedding night, famously visualized as the dropped blanket of prohibition signifying the unseen embrace. However, the title could mean, more innocently, the moment Peter decides to return to New York, reclaim his job, and become a proper suitor for Ellie. Rowe thinks what happened one night was the "realization of Peter's dream" in the night under the stars in the field (1995: 132). Cavell claims the title signifies the willingness to be open to love because "to make things happen, you must let them happen" (1981: 109). In short, the title is not quite a double entendre, but it is available to both innocuous and suggestive readings.

The teasing title points to the strategies by which the studio system of that era could represent sex and produce sexiness while still remaining within the film censorship guidelines that had evolved through the 1920s. *It Happened One Night* is significant as a movie made exactly at the moment when social pressures were mounting toward stricter film censorship in the early 1930s. Shot late in 1933 under the regulations of the 1930 Production Code, it was released in January 1934, four months before more rigorous Code enforcements were implemented. As Shumway points out, the handling of sexual innuendo and desire in *It Happened One Night* became a template for ways in which sex could be handled during the Code era, which stretched over the next several decades (2003: 88). *It Happened One Night* worked as that template because it appropriated the codes and conventions used by filmmakers to depict sexual material so imaginatively under the film industry's self-censorship. This chapter draws on cultural theories of sexuality to explore how the history of censorship shaped the sexual content of *It Happened One Night* and provided a durable formula for the depiction of sex in the romantic comedy film.

As the nuances of its title suggest, the sexiness of *It Happened One Night* is generated by what could *not* be seen or said. As early as 1909, the film industry began self-regulation with respect to sexual content. In the early twentieth century, movies were a primary site of a new cultural frankness about sexuality and a refutation of Victorian decorum about sexual relations. During this time, a resurgent women's movement mobilized not only for suffrage but for birth control (condoms and early versions of the diaphragm), which had became more widely available. Informed by the new field of sexology and the body of scholarship by Havelock Ellis and others, women who defined themselves as feminists – a term first used around 1913 – spoke openly of female sexual desire. By the end of the 1920s, new concepts of sexuality were also being circulated through the promulgation of the idea of companionate marriage and the eroticization of consumer culture, as the promise of sexual attractiveness was being built into the booming business of advertising. The new discourses and concepts included sexual pleasure in marriage, the detachment of sex from procreation, and opportunities for sexual experimentation outside of marriage.

Sexology also named and made visible homosexuality. Self-identified homosexual men and women began to form subcultures, mostly in large cities, by the 1920s. Claudette Colbert herself was rumored to be part of the Hollywood gay subculture which was mostly still invisible to the outside world in the 1930s (see chapter 4). In *It Happened One*

Night, homosexuality is casually referenced by the inclusion of an effeminate sailor who flamboyantly sings a gay-nuanced verse of a well-known song during one of the bus scenes. For at least some members of the contemporary audience, the sailor with a high voice on a bus headed to New York would have had obvious meanings. The sailor had become an urban icon of gay masculinity because of homosexual activity around the New York waterfront, as reflected in the painting *The Fleet's In* (1934) by gay artist Paul Cadmus (Chauncey, 1994: 54, 76–9). In one of the bus scenes of *It Happened One Night,* the entire crowd sings along to "The Man on the Flying Trapeze," a popular song from the nineteenth century about a circus acrobat who steals away the singer's girlfriend. When the sailor offers to sing a verse, he changes the pronoun in the lyrics. Fluttering his hands, he sings of how the trapeze artist one night "smiled on my love" and "blew him a kiss," making the beloved shout "Bravo!" This over-the-top performance was possible because it was coded as sissy comedy, a permissible convention. "By 1933 censor-proof insinuation had become an art form," Vito Russo writes of the representation of homosexuality in movies of this era, and so "the explicitly homosexual sissy flourished" (1987: 40).

Growing urbanization from 1910 to 1930, which made the gay sub-culture possible, also transformed heterosexual relationships between unmarried young people, who moved from spending time together in tightly chaperoned church and family events to public entertainments such as amusement parks, movie theaters, and night clubs. Traditional courtship, consisting of men "calling on" women at home, was replaced by the new practice of dating, which took place in these public places. Dating also escalated sexual activity because it implied that men paid for dinners and entertainment in return for the sexual "favors" of "necking" and "petting" (Bailey, 1989: 15–24; Shumway, 2003: 63–4). In the short story "Night Bus," on which *It Happened One Night* was based, the character of Elspeth exhibits the new modern casualness toward relationships between the sexes, including the possibility that she is sexually experienced. Interactions between men and women were also altered by the growing number of women in the workforce, albeit mostly in lower-paying jobs. Working women, in turn, were the target of the newly vitalized consumerism which encouraged sexual attractiveness through the purchase of cosmetics, clothing, and accessories. In all, sexual topics and desires were more candidly represented and were commodified by emerging entertainments such as motion pictures.

Given these rapid changes in attitudes toward sexuality, by the second decade of the century, filmmakers had learned the box office appeal of racy plots and sexy stars. Audiences flocked to stories involving prostitutes, white slavery, and adultery. Sex comedies such as *Why Change Your Wife?* (1920) were major hits. Filmmakers also promoted stars like Theda Bara, the sensuous vamp in films like *The Devil's Daughter* (1915) and *The Tiger Woman* (1917). Because of shenanigans on-screen and in the lives of the stars, "Hollywood" become a short-hand for sex and depraved morality. Scandals among actors and actresses included the rape and murder conviction of Fatty Arbuckle in 1921; the divorce case that implicated "America's sweetheart" Mary Pickford in adultery in 1920; and rumors of drugs involved in the death of Olive Thomas in 1920. Hollywood became synonymous with vice, so state and municipal censorship boards nationwide began to cut and edit the films shown within their jurisdiction, and church groups threatened boycotts. Rather than deal with external censorship and the loss of audiences, the film industry in 1922 formed the Motion Picture Producers and Distributors Association (MPPDA), administered by Will H. Hays (the Hays Office), to promote self-regulation. However, pressure from the MPPDA couldn't compete with the box office returns of films like *The Merry Widow* (1925), which included an orgy and foot fetishism, and *The Temptress* (1926), featuring Greta Garbo as the mistress of several men (Pennington, 2007: 4–6).

In the hope of becoming more effective, in 1927 the Hayes Office organized a Studio Relations Committee (the SRC) to monitor scripts and register objections. Most importantly, the Hays Office produced a set of guidelines prefaced with principles that proclaimed "the moral importance" of entertainment. The guidelines went into detail about plots, topics, language, and objects that were allowed, forbidden, or discouraged. This was the Motion Picture Production Code of 1930, which remained in effect until 1968.[1]

Sexuality was the issue most scrupulously policed. The Code covered representations of crime, violence, religion, drugs, and alcohol, but almost half of the document is devoted to sexual topics: love triangles, seduction, rape, scenes of passion, "impure love," "lustful embraces," "prolonged kissing," "the nude or semi-nude body," obscene dances and dancing costumes, brothels and bedrooms. Some representations, such as "sex perversion," white slavery, "miscegenation (sex relationships between the white and black races)," and illegal drug trafficking were altogether forbidden, while other topics (brutality, surgery) had to be treated carefully or avoided.

Nevertheless, until 1934, there was no serious industrial enforcement of the guidelines . Producers could appeal to a group comprised of fellow producers who usually sided with their own. As a result, the studios continued to make bedroom comedies, fallen-woman films, brutal gangster flicks, and adultery-ridden melodramas – "pretty much the raw stuff of American culture," as one critic has described these "pre-Code" offerings (Doherty, 1999: 3). Also, the Code had been set up with the expectation that movies would always portray a certain amount of sex and violence; the object had never been to ban them entirely but rather to control how they were portrayed (Sklar, 1975: 174). As a result, in many ways the guidelines invited infractions, and filmmakers worked creatively around the rules. For example, while nudity was forbidden, undressing scenes were not: the stipulation was that undressing scenes be "avoided" except where "necessary for the plot." As film historian Jody Pennington points out, this loophole gave directors ample opportunity to set up important scenes in bedrooms, where undressing and nudity could be suggested without being seen, because "Nudity unseen was better than no nudity at all" (2007: 7).

Given this particular censorship guideline and the conventions that resulted from it, *It Happened One Night* could include a highly suggestive portrayal of Ellie stripping off her lingerie behind a makeshift curtain. It was arguably necessary for the plot and even for the "moral importance" encouraged by the Code because it showed that, although Ellie and Peter were sharing a room and preparing for bed, she was able to undress without his seeing her. The result, of course, is a very sexy scene, cleverly delivered well within the guidelines. The *Variety* review claimed that the film shows that "A clean story can be funnier than a dirty one." Capra's film encountered no major opposition from the Studio Relations Committee. According to Richard Maltby, Columbia Pictures was generally cooperative with the 1930 guidelines, and Capra in particular was respected by the SRC as a director "especially adept at handling 'difficult' material 'delicately'" (1998: 133–6).

In 1933, during the time *It Happened One Night* was being planned, written, and shot, social and political events converged to step up the film industry's self-censorship. The Catholic Church had been threatening boycotts that would involve millions of Americans. That year, it formed the National Leagion of Decency and urged church members to take the League pledge condemning "salacious" motion pictures. Meanwhile, a private foundation, the Payne Study and Experiment Fund, had financed a four-year study by social scientists to determine the effect of movies on children. In 1933 the Fund published a best-selling book, *Our Movie-Made Children*, which argued that movies had an immoral influence on the young. Responding to the Payne Study, the United States Congress began work on legislation that would make it a crime to distribute films that were "morally objectionable" (Doherty, 1999: 320–5).

The film industry acted quickly to pre-empt federal oversight. A powerful censorship mechanism was launched in July 1934 to enforce the 1930 guidelines. The Hays Office was replaced by the Production Code Administration, headed by Joseph Breen, with the authority to impose a fine of $25,000 on any filmmaker or theater owner who made, distributed, or exhibited a film that did not have Code approval. The new censorship code had teeth, and American filmmaking for the next 34 years was deeply affected by regulations about what could and could not be seen, said, inferred, or suggested.[2]

Censorship and the Power of "It"

This history seems to suggest that Hollywood censorship is a matter of deleted scenes and forbidden sights and dialogue. It is far more useful, however, to think of censorship as a "constructive force," actively structuring the conventions of telling stories and handling controversial subjects and themes (Jacobs, 1991: 23). Drawing on Michel Foucault's theory of how sexuality is culturally produced and circulated through discourses and bodies, scholars emphasize that, far from stifling the representation of sex in cinema, the Production Code invited and encouraged sexual expression. In fact, Hollywood sexiness in that era was stylized by resistance to Code regulations. The Code forced "sex" on-screen to become "more concentrated, more verbal, more intense" precisely because it could not be more explicit, as critic Leonard Leff explains. "Who raised the 'walls of Jericho' in *It Happened One Night*?" he asks. "Who lowered them? Perhaps the answer to both questions is Joe Breen" (1991: 438). Although Breen headed the Code administration only after July 1934, he was a major force in its earlier organization under Hays. Leff's point is that the blanket wall provokes and generates sexiness instead of repressing it. The famous photo of Ellie and Peter in the flimsily divided bedroom conveys sex and desire precisely because it shows the barrier, not the consummation. The entire genre of the romantic comedy film was built on the dynamic of the comic delay of sex. Sex, in turn, gets "spoken" precisely by its disappearance into the fade-to-black at the end of the film.

Sex is also spoken through the nebulous pronoun "it" in the film's title. The playfulness of the title was typical of pre-Code movie titles that "titillated with indiscretion and misdirection" (Doherty, 1999: 107). Beyond the ambiguities described earlier, the title of *It Happened One Night* was a sly reference to an entire discourse about sex which 1934 audiences would have recognized right away. Just seven years previously, the hit film *It* (1927) had featured Clara Bow as the "It girl," the embodiment of 1920s sex appeal. The film was adapted from Elinor Glyn's popular novella *It*, the story of a shopgirl who pursues and eventually marries the owner of the department store where she works. *It* had been serialized in *Cosmopolitan* magazine earlier in 1927. In the film version, a close-up of a *Cosmopolitan* article shows a sentence defining "it" as "that magnetic 'sex appeal' which is irresistible." The use of quotation marks around the phrase "sex appeal" suggests its novelty. A British romantic novelist, Glyn began to use the term "it" in 1915 and rose to widespread celebrity in the 1920s by

Shortly after this scene on the bus, Peter tells Ellie, "I'm the man you slept on last night." *It Happened One Night* became the template for the handling of sexual themes through visual and verbal wit after the Production Code of 1930 prohibited explicit sexual representation. Courtesy of Photofest.

claiming expertise on sexual relations. Though Glyn's ideas about sex were conservative, her legacy became the rowdy flapper version of "it" embodied by Clara Bow (Landay, 1998: 75–93).

The connection between *It* and *It Happened One Night* involves the depiction of female sexuality. In the earlier film, both male and female characters are shown striving for "it," but the Clara Bow character, a vivacious shopgirl, is clearly the central figuration of both sex appeal and active sexual desire. Her aggressive pursuit of the department-store owner is unabashedly erotic. Yet, like its imprecise title, the film waffles on what middle-class sexuality means for women in 1927. The Bow character cuts up a dress to give it a plunging neckline, for instance, but the entire plot is about her need to appear respectable. She is "both the wild, rapacious New Woman and the morally correct and conservative young lady of the past," a contradiction rooted in anxieties about "the sexual nature of the New Woman's 'It'" (Orgeron, 2003: 93).

The New Woman was a figure who had emerged in the 1890s but who by the 1920s had drawn to herself more urgent and sexually specific meanings because of the shifts in concepts about sex and gender and in behavior in the preceding decades. With all these changes, the erotic dimension of the newly redefined middle- and upper-class woman was a striking and contentious issue (D'Emilio & Freedman, 1988: 233–68). In *It Happened One Night*, Ellie incarnates a more mature and upscale version of the New Woman than the one in *It*, but we find similar contradictions about her sexuality. Her virginity is fetishized, especially in the first motel scene with the construction of the walls of Jericho, often interpreted as a metaphor for the hymen. But her status as a desiring subject is taken seriously in the later motel scene when she parts the divider curtain – implicitly violating her own virginity and social norms of female passivity – to declare her love and needs.

The short story "Night Bus" is far less ambiguous about Elspeth, who boldly demonstrates the sexual savvy of the New Woman. The changes in the adaptation suggest a continuity in Hollywood portrayals of female sexuality from *It* to *It Happened One Night*. The changes may also suggest caution in light of the 1933 atmosphere created by the Payne Fund report and the new Legion of Decency. Certainly the differences between Adams's Elspeth and Capra's Ellie are fundamental to the sharp difference in sexual attitude between the short story and the movie. "Night Bus" is a racy short story because Elspeth and Peter pose as a married couple, sharing tourist cabins and campsites for lack of money as they travel from Florida to New York. However, the ambience of the short story is urbane, and the sexual tension is handled with flippant humor, mostly because of Elspeth's character.

Elspeth is not in the delicate situation of being a virgin bride. She has not yet married King Westley, but her father disapproves of him, so she has run away in order to rendezvous with Westley in New York. Pragmatic and sexually sophisticated, Elspeth is not very concerned about the respectability of the dividing walls of Jericho. One morning, the wind blows the blanket down and, while they notice it, neither Elspeth nor Peter remarks on it. On another night, the walls of Jericho aren't put up at all because it's raining, and a bathrobe, which has been substituted for the blanket, is in the car. Elspeth is the one who dismisses it. "Why bother? It's pouring, too. Let it go. I don't mind if you don't" (Adams, [1933] 1979: 69–70).

The description in "Night Bus" of their first night together and the original construction of the makeshift wall is worth quoting because it shows how radically different were the tone and fetishizing visual strategies adopted in the film. In the short story, when Elspeth realizes that Peter intends to stay in the same room with her, she protests that she knows nothing about him. He challenges her to take a look at him and see if he looks like a "villain." "She began to giggle. 'You look like a plumber. A nice, honest, intelligent, high-principled plumber.'" In the film the plumber reference is used in a different context to denote the working class as both "fun" and sexually charged (as discussed in chapter 1). But in the story, the reference is used, with amusement, to denote the virtue that will allow Peter to share Elspeth's room. When Elspeth returns from the outdoor washroom, Peter has erected the blanket divider:

> "The walls of Jericho," was his explanation, as she came in. "Solid porphyry and marble. Proof against any assault."
>
> "Grand! What's this?" She recoiled a little from a gaudy splotch ornamenting the foot of her bed.
>
> "Pajamas. My spare set. Hope you can sleep in them."
>
> "I could sleep," she averred with conviction, "in a straitjacket." She had an impulse of irrepressible mischief. "About those walls of Jericho, Peter. You haven't got a trumpet in that big valise of yours, have you?"
>
> "Not even a mouth organ."
>
> "I was just going to tell you not to blow it before eight o'clock."
>
> "Oh, shut up and go to sleep."
>
> So they both went to sleep. (Adams, [1933] 1979: 48)

Notice that Elspeth is the one who, with "irrepressible mischief," introduces the idea of a trumpet to take down the wall. This flirtatious and risqué question pushes the implication of the biblical reference.

In the Old Testament book of Joshua, the Israelites attack the city of Jericho and successfully bring down its walls by having the Israelite priests blow their trumpets. As Ed Sikov says of the film version, the allusion means "both sexual combat and the inevitability of its collapse" (1989: 88). So Elspeth is anticipating the breakdown of the wall and is impudently asking if Peter is aroused – if he's "got a trumpet." Peter's reply picks up on the double entendre by denying it but invoking "a mouth organ," the possibility of oral sex. The give and take here is suggestive, two-sided, and coolly grown-up. Confident to the point of smugness, Elspeth takes control of the conversation, steering it into a flirtatious exchange and then a clever follow-up about the trumpet as an alarm clock. Notable, too, is that the sexual comedy relies on witty dialogue and skips entirely the physical details of Elspeth changing clothes, getting into the pajamas, and settling into a bed just a few feet away from Peter's. All this is eclipsed by understatement: "So they both went to sleep."

Constructing the Walls of Jericho

As opposed to the sharp brevity of the "Night Bus" episode, *It Happened One Night* delivers an extended and detailed incident which has become one of the most famous comedy scenes in Hollywood film history. Its fame resides in sexiness produced through spoken and visual wit, innuendo, and restraint. In a shrewd use of *mise en scène*, the blanket divider becomes a prop with multiple uses and symbolic resonances, and the undressing of each character is maximized for visual and comic/dramatic effect. In all, the editing, lighting, and framing produce a scene rich with meaning about the blanket/walls of Jericho, the Freudian implications of the humor, the effects of censorship, and social and economic differences.

Far from the relaxed and witty Elspeth of the short story, Ellie is in much of this scene vulnerable and humorless; in fact, the humor centers on her discomfort – a society girl stranded in a dumpy motel, but also a virgin bride spending the night with a stranger. Unlike Elspeth, whose sexual experience is implied by her casual attitude,

Ellie is visibly unaccustomed to being alone with a man, and her virginity – her status as the bride still waiting for the wedding night – cranks up the stakes on her sexual susceptibility. So the effort to make Ellie a more conservative character produces a far more teasing and highly sexualized scenario.

The motel scene takes place at a moment when Peter and Ellie have become outright antagonists in a battle of the sexes that was to become standard for the romantic comedy film. Their battle is intensified by class antagonism as well. Ellie shows no gratitude to Peter when he tries, unsuccessfully, to catch a thief who has stolen her suitcase during one of the bus rest-stops. Then, during the breakfast stop, Ellie misses the bus because she thinks it will wait for her. Peter is not surprised by her attitude of entitlement because he has matched Ellie to the newspaper photo of the headline story "ELLIE ANDREWS ESCAPES FATHER." She confirms all his stereotypes about rich people when she offers him money, promising to pay him after she gets to New York, instead of simply asking him for help. Peter heatedly expresses his contempt for her as a "spoiled brat" who thinks only in terms of what she can buy. "I'm not interested in you or your problem. You, your father, King Westley, you're all a lot of hooey to me," he says lividly. Unpleasant as Peter has become to her, Ellie repeatedly finds herself in his debt. She doesn't realize she has lost her bus ticket, and Peter is the one who finds it on the seat. Peter has also had to rescue her from the designs of the sleazy fellow passenger Shapeley, which he does by claiming Ellie as his wife. And when Ellie attempts to buy a box of chocolates on the bus, Peter bluntly forbids it, pointing out that, with just a few dollars between them, they need to budget carefully to make it to New York. So the class conflict and gender dynamics – paternal bullying and protection, feminine resentment – set up an especially volatile background for the intimate motel scene.

The bus passengers suddenly learn that the road has been closed because of flooding and rain. Peter jumps out to check out the tourist cabins where the bus has stopped. A wipe designates the beginning of a scene, and then Capra uses a tracking shot, as he had done in the first bus station scene, to make a connection and a narrative point. The shot begins at a modestly designed sign, "Dyke's Auto Camp, $2.00," and crosses the rainy darkness to Ellie wearing Peter's raincoat and smoking a cigarette as she waits under the eaves of the office porch. Aside from the social irony of the heiress at a two-dollar auto camp, the shot indicates that Ellie and her reactions will be the focus of this scene, as the follow-up makes clear. We see Peter and the camp owner exchanging money at a cabin door, and Peter calls over to Ellie that they're all set up. As Ellie makes her way to the cabin, the raincoat over her head to protect her from the rain, the proprietor stops to say, "Good evening. Hope you and your husband rest comfortable." A medium shot focuses on her astounded facial expression, and she looks straight at the camera for a second as the implication hits her. Her father had declared that, though she and Westley were married, they "would never live under the same roof." Now, on a stormy night, she is about to sleep under the same roof with a handsome stranger who has registered them as man and wife. The comedy has shifted from social satire – the debutante at the auto camp – to bedroom satire hooked to the era's contradictory sexual ideology. Ellie may be the spunky New Woman with her cigarette, traveling alone to outsmart her meddling father, but she is also still the respectable 1930s woman defined in conventional ways: a maiden, a virgin, a good girl who does not share sleeping quarters with a strange man.

Unmistakably, the joke is on her, as is evident in the following shots which contrast her shocked face and frozen figure with Peter's dexterous energy as he dashes around the room, getting them settled in and explaining how lucky they were to get a cabin. Ellie remains immobilized at the door, the oversized coat wrapped tightly around herself for protection. In the ensuing conversation, Peter furthers his power leverage, revealing himself as a newspaper reporter with dibs on her story and threatening to alert her father if she doesn't stay. It's blackmail. Her facial expressions subtly register disbelief, then anger, and then a brave attempt to remain dignified as she realizes her choices are either capture by her father or captivity with Peter in the cabin. Ellie's misery stacks the odds against this match, increasing the genre's tension about how this (inevitable) romance will work out. And, in terms of the comedy, her misery signals the conventional moral codes that makes this situation racy.

Peter is openly having fun, beaming and making a point of fussing with the room – checking the softness of one of the mattresses, pulling down a blind – during the first part of this scene. He has falsely registered them as a married couple and forced an heiress to stay at Dyke's Auto Camp. Breaking the rules feeds his bad-boy disposition. But the limits of his bad-boy streak are laid out as well. In the conversation with Ellie, he tells her plainly that she need not worry; he has no interest in her at all except "as a headline." With this assurance, he is free to tease her sense of decorum, and the film is free to tease the limits of decorum as well, pushing against what could be portrayed and inferred in 1933–4 cinema about an unmarried couple sharing a room.

To this end, the script gives Peter a witty monologue and two choice comic routines – the walls of Jericho improvisation and a mock striptease – to show off the brashness of both the character and the film. When it becomes obvious that Ellie has no choice except to stay, he cheerfully throws a blanket over a clothes line that he has strung through the middle of the room between the two beds. "That, I suppose, makes everything quite alright," Ellie says drily. Backed stiffly against the door, she eyes Peter with grim suspicion as he launches into a satirical riff about the blanket as the walls of Jericho, followed by a game of "chicken" as he undresses – that is, he removes his clothing piece by piece, daring her to stay until the moment he takes off his trousers.

Peter's opening scenes have established how much he enjoys performing in front of an audience, and his improvisation here is a send-up of propriety. He has put up the blanket wall, he tells her coyly, to protect his own modesty: "I like privacy when I retire. Yes, I'm very delicate in that respect. Prying eyes annoy me." The comic reversal, the implication that she would be the one to "pry," is registered in a reverse shot showing embarrassment and irritation pass over Ellie's face. In the same mocking tone, Peter alludes to the biblical story: "Behold the walls of Jericho. Maybe not as thick as the ones Joshua blew down, but a lot safer. For you

The composition of this publicity shot, which shows Ellie and Peter separated by a flimsy blanket (the "walls of Jericho") in a motel room, suggests both sexual tension and the many divisions between them. Courtesy of Photofest.

see, I have no trumpet." Smiling and effusive, Peter illustrates his speech with theatrical gestures, holding up the blanket to illustrate its substance and plucking at his sweater like a magician to prove there is in fact no trumpet up his sleeve. In reverse shots, Ellie's expressions indicate her growing discomfort. Continuing the joke that she, not he, is the potential aggressor, he gestures to her side of the blanket and asks her to "join the Israelites" so he can prepare for bed. As Cavell points out, Peter's characterization of Ellie as an attacking Israelite suggests that "whether the walls come down will depend on whether the right sounds issue from her side of the wall" (1981: 81).

In a gesture of pure defiance, and against the conventions of modesty, Ellie stubbornly refuses to move. This begins the film's celebrated striptease – both humorous and aggressive – performed by Peter. The striptease is a power play between two highly willful people, and what's at stake is no less than the male body and its potential sexual threat. Ellie's refusal to follow his orders and go to her side of the room (like a good girl) amounts to calling his bluff. His response is to call *her* bluff to see how long she will stick around to witness what can or cannot be seen of his sexual power. Peter's monologue makes the game funny, but the flip side is the danger of sexual power relations – the male power of rape and Ellie's vulnerability.

A medium shot squares them off against each other in one long take, Peter on the left in front of the blanket wall, Ellie on the right, leaning against the door watching him, clutching to her chest the pair of men's pajamas he'd tossed her. "Perhaps you're interested in how a man undresses," he says with enthusiasm as he slips out of his pullover sweater. She refuses to budge or even look alarmed as he takes off his tie, shirt, and shoes. Peter, in turn, punctuates his disrobing with a mocking lecture on the various ways men undress. The removal of the shirt reveals bare skin, a move that supposedly sent the sales of men's undershirts plummeting for a decade. Not until he reaches for his belt buckle does Ellie duck her head and scurry to the other side of the blanket, where the privacy of the divider allows her to wince with disgust and angrily throw his pajamas on the bed.

The syntax of the next set of shots indicates the seriousness of her situation. With a swiftness that looks like desperation, Ellie goes to the window and lifts the shade. A shot from outside positions her within the window frame, trapped by the pouring rain, the isolation of the cabin, and the wiliness of her roommate. She looks in all directions as if figuring her chances of escape, and then glumly turns away, resigned to a night with Peter. But she is also resigned to her loss in the power struggle against Peter's masculine advantage and manipulation.

The next shot emphasizes the difference in their perspectives. On his side of the blanket, Peter wears a black dressing gown and smokes a cigarette, casually advising her not to "be a sucker" and to get a good night's sleep. He also offers one last taunt: "The walls of Jericho will protect you from the big bad wolf." Settling into bed with his cigarette, he sings a version of a song instantly familiar to the film's contemporary audience, "Who's Afraid of the Big Bad Wolf?" It is the theme song from Walt Disney's highly successful cartoon short "The Three

Little Pigs" (1933) which was so popular that the song had become a national hit (Sklar, 1975: 204). For 1934 audiences, its sudden appearance in a highly charged sexual scenario would have been especially funny. It also would have aligned Peter with popular culture and thus further away from the set of values associated with Ellie – the yacht, the aviator fiancé, the sense of entitlement that makes her think a Greyhound bus will wait for her during one of its scheduled stops.

Peter's glib humor during this monologue – beginning with his prattling about the walls of Jericho and ending with the taunting little song – was no doubt what made this scene possible in 1930s cinema. The erotic charge of the small motel room, the beds, and a man undressing in front of a woman are tempered by the lightness of his fast talk. But the humor also grows more aggressive during the monologue, from Peter's coy assertion of his own "delicate" modesty to the outright taunt of the Disney song. The aggressiveness escalates exactly to the measure of increased physical intimacy through this scene, first the construction of the wall which places Ellie on *his* side of the room, then the disrobing, and then Peter in his bed continuing the conversation so that the flimsiness of the "wall" is emphasized.

So the humor, a defensive gesture against censorship, is also an offensive gesture in relation to its target, Ellie. The offensiveness or aggression is phallic, as suggested by Peter's joke about his lack of a trumpet. Peter can joke about his "lack" because phallic power is larger than the phallus, as indicated by the goading song about the "big bad wolf," which characterizes Ellie as besieged and needing protection against a large, voracious animal with enormous teeth. Peter's threat has "teeth" not only because of the power of rape, but because he has outwitted Ellie into needing his cooperation and has proven himself to be a capable masculine protector. In this scene, Peter's cockiness – there is no other word for it – also reflects his pleasure at the inverted social relations: the powerlessness of the heiress, the power of the unemployed average guy.

Sigmund Freud claims that jokes that are not "innocent" are either "hostile" or "obscene," and Peter's monologue falls within both of the latter categories. The hostile joke, says Freud, "will allow us to exploit something ridiculous in our enemy which we could not … bring forward openly or consciously" (1960: 103). When Peter feigns fussiness with the drab motel accommodation and the wall that protects his "delicate" sensitivity, he is venting his class hostility toward the "spoiled brat" and the bourgeois conventions she values. The joke here is shared by the film's visual dynamics in the tracking shot from "Dyke's Auto Camp" to the imperious Ellie and in the framing of the contrast between Ellie's frozen demeanor and Peter's boyish rambunctiousness.

The result of this hostility is the silencing of Ellie in this portion of the scene. The bold New Woman has clearly been put in her place. After her ironic remark about the blanket wall making "everything quite alright," she has no lines for more than three minutes, while Peter is doing the walls of Jericho and striptease routines. Having been forced to her side of the blanket wall, she broods about the hope-lessness of her situation, and the only sound is the constant torrent of rain against the windows. She is silent for so long, in fact, that Peter asks, "Still with me, brat?" If Peter is waiting for "the right sounds" from her side of the Jericho wall, she is signaling that the barrier is still in place – the sexual barrier, the class barrier, the personality barrier between two stubborn people. The silencing of Ellie here is also evidence for the darker interpretations of the gender dynamics of this film, such as Maltby's (1998) reading of *It Happened One Night* as patriarchal reclamation of the defiant woman.

However, the other effect of Peter's monologue and striptease is the awakening of Ellie's sexual desire. In Freud's analysis of the "obscene" joke or "smut," the joke "is directed to a particular person, by whom one is sexually excited and who, on hearing it, is expected to become aware of the speaker's excitement and as a result to become sexually excited in turn" (1960: 97). So the sexual innuendoes of Peter's humor work on two levels. He "uses the threat of sex (his strip routine) to prevent sex (by making Ellie run for her modesty)," as one critic points out (Poague, 1974: 157). But the strip routine and the follow-up ditty about the "big bad wolf" are an enticement to sex as well. The bare chest and taunting song are sexually aggressive, and the remainder of the scene suggests they are effective in having their female target "become sexually excited in turn."

The visual and sexual dynamics suddenly change. Whereas the camera had previously positioned Ellie as the target of Peter's bad-boy humor, she is now positioned as complicit in prohibited desire. Shot/ reverse shots emphasize both their separation and their physical proximity. Even more importantly, the lighting changes. Preparing to undress in the small space on her side of the blanket, Ellie asks Peter to put out the light. The concession to modesty results in romantic backlighting, with the light (supposedly moonlight) coming in from the window above each bed. Each character becomes a silhouette against the moonlight, the windows awash in rain, the shadows playing with their faces as Peter settles more comfortably into the mattress and Ellie begins to undress.

In contrast to Peter's brash striptease, Ellie's undressing is far more seriously eroticized. Peter's disrobing took place in full lighting with a medium shot showing most of his body. With Ellie, the lights are dimmed, and her body is glimpsed only in silhouette and in parts, mostly from the shoulder up, rather than revealed in full. So her body is fetishized by framing and editing that arouse curiosity, a long-standing Hollywood convention regarding the representation of female sexuality. Peter stood in front of Ellie with nothing between them, but for Ellie's undressing, the blanket barrier impedes what Peter can see, so the act is far more provocative.

Cavell suggests that the walls of Jericho, as a big clunky barricade, parody the Production Code. The blanket inspires "an erotic reaction" because it works the way censorship does, by "activating our imagination." It parodies censorship's detailed list of prohibited objects and scenarios by using a simple blanket as the focus of sexual agitation (1981: 82–3). Evidence of its suggestiveness is that Ohio's censorship board ordered the cutting of "all scenes where blanket is shown [*sic*]" (Maltby 1998: 136). In Foucauldian terms, sexiness is produced by the very mechanisms that limit and proscribe it.

For Peter, the effect of Ellie's unseen actions behind the blanket is made clear. A close-up shows him in bed, suddenly very quiet and interested in what he sees. An eyeline shot reveals the blanket moving with Ellie's body moving against it. Then a piece of lingerie, and then another piece, is hung over the top from Ellie's side. "I wish you'd take those things off the walls of Jericho," he says in a subdued voice. His earlier mocking tone is gone. The shot returns to the blanket.

We hear her quick apology and the "things" slip out of sight. What had apparently been, for Ellie, an impromptu clothes line is transformed into a line of sexual provocation. The question is whether or not Ellie's gesture is as innocent as it seems. Is the rich girl leaving her discarded clothing wherever she wants, or is this an unconscious tease for the man on the other side?

What follows, in absolute silence, are two shot/reverse shots of Peter very still in bed and Ellie in silhouette, shrugging on the pajamas and then climbing into bed. Sexual tension is palpable in the silence, the syntax of the editing, and the backlighting which outlines their figures as smoky silhouettes. The critic Barbara Bowman points out how the film spectator's implication in the visual arrangement intensifies the eroticism of the scene. The blanket barrier between the two characters positions us, as voyeurs, in a different way from most erotic scenes. "The eyes and the exchanged glances that usually inform such a scene become ours: the film spectator becomes a mediator between Peter and Ellie" (1992: 39).

The scene could have ended there, with the sexual chemistry clearly established by these cinematic codes. Instead, it ends with a conversation – the ironic, teasing dialogue that became the signature of romantic comedy, in part because of the growing sophistication of sound systems in the 1930s and in part because of the censorship pressures that made sex "more verbal," as Leff (1991) points out. It's pillow talk, but pillow talk through a blanket between separate beds, a scenario that is both erotic and comic, shown in shot/reverse shots between the two shadowy figures.[3] The dialogue shows that Peter and Ellie have left behind their earlier hostility and are moving toward a new kind of relationship, both intimate and wary, which will typify romantic comedy couples for generations to come.

It begins when Ellie suddenly sits up, apparently realizing she is sharing a room with a man whose name she doesn't know. When she asks who he is, Peter responds with elusive poetry. "Who, me? I'm the whippoorwill that cries in the night. I'm the soft morning breeze that caresses your lovely face." The sardonic tone this time seems to be self-mockery rather than sarcasm aimed at Ellie. Even in the darkness, we can discern the softening of their faces into barely suppressed smiles. Peter gives his name at Ellie's insistence, and she considers it for a moment before making a plucky reply: "Peter Warne. I don't like it." As James Harvey points out, this surprising comment shows that Ellie now feels on an equal footing with Peter. The retort is "her version of brashness: a reversal, witty and unexpected" (1987: 113). This initiates a short comic exchange about how, as a woman taking her husband's name, she does not need to keep it beyond the morning. "Pleased to meet you, Mr. Warne," she concludes. "The pleasure is all mine … Mrs. Warne," Peter responds. Just as the walls of Jericho are erected precisely so they can be torn down, the mocking use of the married name foreshadows the inevitable marriage.

This is the spirited give and take of romantic comedy, taut with sexual overtones about their masquerade as a married couple and overlaid with irony as each character keeps his or her distance. A visual coda follows Peter's remark, beginning with a reverse shot of the silhouetted figure of Ellie in bed, a light glinting just briefly in her eyes as she settles herself into the pillow. For Harvey, the shot "connects wit and yearning, going from little smiles on each side of the curtain to the gleam in the heroine's eye" (1987: 112). The final shot of the scene reinforces the *mise en scène* of desire; the shot is framed to show both beds, the room split by the blanket barrier, the light streaming in from the window above each bed.

The shot lingers for a full five seconds on this dark, divided room, the walls of Jericho looming between would-be lovers. The give and take of the conversation has redrawn this dividing line to signify more than the incitement and prohibition of sex. Ellie and Peter are clearly attracted to each other, but the barriers between them are social, psychological, ideological, and circumstantial. The most obvious narrative obstacle is Ellie's marriage to Westley, but they are also deeply divided by class and by the attitudes generated by class difference. So the walls of Jericho can be interpreted as an icon of screwball comedy and its class divisions which will be overcome by romance (Bergman, 1971: 137). Although the ensuing narrative makes her humbler, Ellie has so far shown not only the careless arrogance of the wealthy (e.g., expecting the Greyhound bus to wait for her) but also the assumption that everyone's motivations are monetary (e.g., offering Peter a future reward for his help). Peter's stereotyping of Ellie as a rich, spoiled brat continues to blind him through most of the narrative, even after Ellie proves herself a far more complex and generous person. Given Peter's cynicism and blindness, Cavell argues that the divider wall symbolizes the larger, metaphysical separation of souls: "What it censors is the man's knowledge of the existence of the human being 'on the other side'" (1981: 109).[4]

The walls of Jericho have generated varying interpretations of their sexual meanings. As we saw in chapter 1, Rowe reads the walls of Jericho as an empowering symbol for Ellie because they so blatantly represents the hymen and thus the virginity that allows Ellie her independence. So long as Ellie remains a virgin, despite her marriage to Westley, she retains some agency (1995: 128–9). This interpretation extends the blanket wall as sexual prohibition into a narrative meaning about the power of the romantic heroine. For Shumway, focusing on the illusions about marriage promulgated by romantic comedy, the meaning of the barrier blanket resides in its flimsiness as a pretext for the night in the motel: Ellie is a married woman and the episode's implication is adultery. "We are meant to understand their 'sleeping together' separated by these 'walls of Jericho' as an adulterous adventure even if the night is literally chaste" (2003: 90–1). The "adulterous" thrill of the night together leads to marriage, according to Shumway, even though marriage cannot possibly sustain this kind of thrill.

The enormous differences among these interpretations – the walls of Jericho signifying virginity or adultery, censorship or its parody, class difference or metaphysical isolation – suggest not only very different reading agendas, but also the richness of this icon, which keeps generating meanings about relations between the sexes as well as relations between these two fictional characters.

The Walls Tumble Down

This richness continues the second time the walls appear, much later in the film, during the final night of the journey, at a second motel cabin. By this time, Peter and Ellie have bonded as a couple sharing an adventure on the road, in good times and bad. They have had fun singing with the other passengers on the bus, and Ellie has proven herself to be better than Peter at getting a ride from a passing car. The driver of that car has tried to steal their suitcase, and in turn Peter has stolen the car. Most importantly, they have acknowledged their romantic attraction to each other when they spent the night in a hayfield under the stars. Bending over Ellie to make a bed of hay for her, Peter was poised to kiss her, and Ellie was obviously ready and willing to be kissed. But the rules of censorship and of the romantic genre intrude. According to the 1930 Code, Ellie is a married woman and the kiss would have shown "impure love." And according to the rules of romantic comedy (which this very film was developing) the narrative first needs to solve the problem of her first marriage.

Ellie's marriage to Westley weighs in heavily in the second motel scene when Peter again constructs the blanket wall. Watching this, Ellie asks Peter if she'll see him in New York. He says no and explains curtly, "I don't make it a policy to run around with married women." The setting of this exchange – both of them undressing in a small motel room – certainly suggests adultery. Yet the wall barrier as Ellie's power of virginity is also at play here; as Rowe (1995) points out, Ellie uses her liminal status to expand the story and delay the ending by insisting that they stop at the motel even though they are only a few hours from New York. She even hides from Peter a newspaper which announces in a giant headline that her father has forgiven her and welcomes her back to join her husband. So Ellie is the manipulator of this scene, which is necessary to change the ending of the story, or "to make things happen."

The tone of this scene differs dramatically from the first motel scene. Peter's gleeful bad-boy flippancy is entirely gone, and the actions that had been so titillating in the earlier scene – the building of the walls, the undressing of Peter and Ellie – are now done in the silence of unhappy sexual frustration. On the one hand, as Cavell (1981) notes, they are "living under the same roof" with the matter-of-factness of long-married couples. Ellie watches without comment as Peter rigs up the blanket wall, and she absent-mindedly smooths out a fold so it hangs evenly. On the other hand, they are making an outrageous arrangement which no married couple would make, separating themselves out of each other's range of vision. Unlike the earlier scene which had positioned the beds on opposite sides of the frame, the framing here gives us at first both beds on the same side, suggesting this couple is by now not nearly as divided as domestically joined. The cinematography is different too, the lighting producing rich and complex shadows giving the effect of depth which cues the drama of this scene compared to the humor of the earlier one.

The bitter irony of their situation is summed up by their opening dialogue, when Peter glumly points out that by morning she'll be in the arms of her husband, and Ellie points out in return that he'll have a "great story." Each dejectedly agrees. This was their bargain, reached within a tense power struggle at the start of their night at Dyke's Auto Camp. Forty-eight hours later, the achievement of both goals has made them miserable. When Ellie presses the point about wanting to see him again, Peter's reply is angry. He asks sharply why she would want to see him after he's served his purpose of bringing her back to King Westley. "That's what you wanted, wasn't it?" We see him slam down the pillow before he gets into his bed.

The blanket wall has shifted in meaning just as the shared, divided room has shifted in meaning, from sexual thrill and danger to the frustrated separation of a couple in love. An element of absurdity colors the *mise en scène* of this conversation because, through most of it, Ellie faces away from the camera and speaks to the blanket as she undresses and sits on the bed. However, the framing changes to suggest a possible alteration of their relationship. Following Peter's cross reply, the next shot shows both beds with the blanket between them. But unlike the famous shot in the earlier motel scene, the blanket does not split the frame. Instead, we see it at three-quarters length, framed from Ellie's side of the room. That is, it shows a way around the blanket. In fact, it shows how easily the blanket could be side-stepped. Peter is in his bed, angrily resigned about Ellie's return to her husband. But Ellie sits on the edge of her bed in his pajamas, hugging herself and leaning toward the blanket, her entire body tense with longing and anticipation. Unlike Peter, she is not yet resigned to the inevitable end of her own journey.

At this key moment in the narrative, Ellie insists not only on conversation – the touchstone of romantic comedy – but on an *intimate* conversation, pushing for a connection between herself and Peter despite the divider blanket and despite Peter's grumpiness. As Shumway reminds us, in the first third of the twentieth century the discourse of intimacy was fairly new as an expectation for couples. In contrast to the "adventure" and intensity of romance, intimacy involves "communication, friendship, and sharing that will last beyond the passion of new love" (2003: 27). Ellie's intimate question to Peter is whether he's ever been in love, and his reply is significant because it shows that, for all his bluster and macho posturing, he is capable of intimate discourse.

Peter's speech reveals his vulnerability and his disappointment at being "a sucker" in trying to find "somebody that's real, somebody that's alive." Ironically, it also exposes his blindness about his own situation. He has had overwhelming evidence in the previous two days that Ellie is just such a "real" and "alive" woman – a good sport about their hardships, spunky enough to flash a leg to get a ride, generous enough to give away their last dollar to a hungry kid on the bus. Likewise, he describes his island in the Pacific as the site of moonlit nights when the stars are close and "you feel that you're part of something big and marvelous," seemingly oblivious to the fact that he and Ellie have shared just such a moonlit experience the previous night. In Cavell's view, Peter has problems connecting the ideal to the real, "connecting the woman's body and soul … his perception and his imagination" (1981: 109).

Reverse shots show the passionate effect of this speech on Ellie, who listens in anguish as Peter describes the ideal woman he has yet to find. His words have a physical impact on her: we see her breath coming quickly, and at one point she arches back on the bed as if crushed by Peter's inability to see her as the "real" woman he would take to the island. Her arched back also signifies palpable sexual longing. We are seeing a woman who openly and physically desires the man on the other side of the room. The camera returns to Peter wrapping up his speech. "Boy, if I could ever find a girl who's hungry for those th—"

Peter does not complete his thought because he is stopped cold by what he sees off-frame. The eyeline shot delivers a shocking sight: Ellie in pajamas, her eyes brimming with tears, pulling aside the blanket barrier and everything it stands for – sexual prohibition, psychological separation, class division, the censorship of feelings and desires. Of Ellie's three plot-changing initiatives in this film, this indiscretion in the motel cabin is the bravest and most risky. Her earlier dive from the yacht was gutsy but the worst that could have happened was recapture by an intrusive but doting father. Similarly, her later dash across the lawn as the runaway bride makes for dramatic footage, but it's an action her father has sanctioned and helped to prepare. In contrast, her transgression of the blanket divider is an enormous personal gamble and a scandalous transgression of patriarchal codes.

Describing her action to her father later, Ellie says, "I threw myself at him." This is no small act in terms of the trajectory of the story and the larger cultural trajectory of female sexuality. Ellie's modesty and virginity had been established in the first motel scene. This character is not one of the early 1930s Hollywood bombshells but a woman for whom sexual integrity has meaning. Rowe (1995) argues that Ellie's virginity is her power, affording her the advantage of remaining outside the law that would make her subject to a man. Hazarding her virginity while technically still married to King Westley, Ellie is gambling away this power. She is also defying the patriarchal code in which female virginity has value in relation to male authority.

Most of all, she is risking the loss of Peter, who has been established as a man deeply respectful of bourgeois values, despite his bad-boy taunts at Dyke's Auto Camp. Maltby calls him "an archetype of middle-class male normality" (1998: 156). Harvey argues that the hitchhiking incident had revealed Peter's essential conservative nature: by lifting her skirt to get the ride, Ellie "goes further than he ever could; she is unconventional and he is not" (1987: 117). After all, Peter's grouchiness in this motel scene is rooted in his "understanding among men about property: on paper, Ellie belongs to King Westley" (Rowe, 1995: 133). Ellie's transgression is also a clue to the importance of romantic comedy for women. The genre emphasizes female desire as well as love; the would-be lover must be chosen by the heroine. "Thus it is not a coincidence that Clark Gable begins a striptease for Claudette Colbert or that it is she who first breaches the walls," Shumway points out (2003: 92).

Given the specific meanings of the walls of Jericho as set up by Peter himself in the earlier scene – the goading about the big bad wolf, the teasing about her defenselessness – Ellie's breach of the wall throws away her safety and virtue. The moral implications of this are tempered by the cinematography. First, a medium shot shows her appearance at the edge of the blanket. Then a close-up uses soft focus for a far more romantic effect. While the rest of the scene had used deep focus to produce sharp shadows, we now see Ellie's face, her eyes shining with tears, in the softening haze that codes the romantic heroine. But while the soft focus says romance rather than sex, Ellie's speech is not as elliptical. The next shot shows her from behind, kneeling at Peter's bed, and we hear her voice, heaving with passion: "Take me with you, Peter. Take me to your island. I want to do all those things you talked about." When he tells her firmly she better go back to her bed, she puts her hand on his chest to emphasize her meaning. "I love you. Nothing else matters. We can run away. Everything else will take care of itself. Please, Peter. I can't let you out of my life now. I couldn't live without you."

The sexual inferences of this are clear. When Ellie sums up Peter's description of the stars, night, and surf as "all those things" he talked about, she is reading those "things" as sexual passion. She has flung herself onto him on the bed, and she would no doubt climb into it if he gave the word. Again, the limits of cultural narrative (this is a good girl, after all) and of film censorship (Columbia Pictures' cooperation with the Hays Office) shape the only possible outcome of Ellie's action. When Ellie's speech turns into a sobbing plea – "Please, Peter," he puts his arm around her and they embrace while she sobs into his chest. A kiss during this bed scene would have crossed the line. Instead, Peter gently but firmly tells her a second time, "You better go back to your bed."

The resulting confusion and complications follow the pattern in Shakespeare's comedies, where would-be lovers are separated by coincidences, misunderstandings, and subplots that delay their union. Peter decides to go back to New York in the middle of the night, recover his job, and presumably return with a proposal for Ellie before she awakens. The comic mini-subplot here involves the owner of the motel cabins and his nagging wife, who has already made a brief appearance to berate her husband about his trust of strangers who promise to pay later. By coincidence, Ma has taken milk of magnesia, which wakes her in time to hear Peter's car pull away. Ma rouses Zeke out of bed to tell him triumphantly that they've indeed been cheated.

They bustle down to the cabin to wake Ellie and inform her that her husband – "if he *is* your husband," Ma says archly – is gone. Ellie is left to believe she has been deserted as a result of her impulsive breach of the divider wall and her passionate speech to Peter.

When Zeke and Ma break into the cabin, the bumbling Zeke pulls down the walls of Jericho as part of the grim exposure of deceit and indecency. Following the intense scene of sexual frustration which the walls had symbolized, this is a wicked comic touch. Ma and Zeke are comic representatives of the forces of morality because they so drastically misread the scene. They understand neither the innocence of what they see – a woman left alone in a motel room – nor the eroticism of what they have just casually thrown aside – the blanket. In a film made at a time when censorship and questions of morality on-screen loomed large, the frumpy motel owners parody the entire process of censorship, suggesting the futility of designating certain scenarios or objects as inherently indecent. The motel sequence ends with Ma scolding Ellie as the latter is unceremoniously being evicted. "Next time you better not come back here," Ma calls after her. "I run a respectable place." We want to call back to her, "But nothing happened!" Yet it would be difficult to argue that nothing at all happened that night.

Chapter 3

Capra, Class, and the Runaway Heiress

Hollywood and the Great Depression

During the bus journey in *It Happened One Night*, a woman passenger faints from hunger. Her weeping son explains that they'd spent all their money on bus tickets so they could get to New York because his mother had been promised a job there. In one sense, the incident is not about these hungry passengers so much as about the main characters, Peter and Ellie, and their development as a couple. Without hesitation, Ellie gives the boy their last dollar. Peter's surprise at this suggests that he may not have been so generous himself, but he quickly rallies to support Ellie's benevolence. When the boy tries to give back the money, Peter brushes it off with "Nah, I've got millions."

The loss of this dollar actually means hunger for Ellie and Peter, who for an entire day have nothing to eat except some carrots Peter has dug up from a field. The need for food is developed as a metaphor throughout the film (as described in chapter 1), designating emotional, erotic, and metaphysical yearning. But hunger in *It Happened One Night* is also an important historical reference. When the film was released early in 1934, its audience had experienced the worst of the Great Depression, which had begun in 1929. President Herbert Hoover famously declared in 1932 that no one was actually starving, but in the following year, in New York City alone, there were 29 recorded deaths due to starvation and in 1934 there were 110. The national statistics on deaths due to starvation are unacknowledged because malnutrition caused so many other fatal complications. There is documentation of families digging in garbage dumps in large cities during this time (Kyving, 2002: 226). For about half of the nation's workers, cutbacks and underemployment meant hardship and adversity. Without doubt, many people who saw this film in 1934 would have read the fainting woman as a marker of realism – no father in sight, mother as wage earner, traveling penniless – in a fantasy about an heiress who refuses a steak dinner and runs away on a bus.

The historical contexts of *It Happened One Night* are crucial for an understanding of the issues raised by the fainting passenger and the Andrews family lifestyle. After all, given the widespread destitution of the early 1930s, why would an audience be interested in an heiress on a hunger strike? How could Capra get away with a yacht-owning millionaire who turns out to have a heart of gold? For that matter, how could movies survive in the Depression, not only as a commodity but as an entertainment form that in some way registered "reality," when reality was so grim?

In addition, the historical context of *It Happened One Night* grounds the very different interpretations of its treatment of gender and romance discussed in chapter 1. Maltby interprets the Depression as a severely emasculating experience for American men who could no longer provide for their families. This is his basis for reading *It Happened One Night* as a film that restores patriarchal authority by redeeming Mr. Andrews and aligning him with Peter; both of them together know what's best for the errant daughter (1998: 155). Kendall regards the Depression as having had the opposite effect. She sees *It Happened One Night* as the beginning of "Depression romantic comedy," which appealed to disillusioned audiences through "a feisty but also vulnerable heroine" and through the promotion of "feminine" values – "a moral subtlety, an unashamed belief in the validity of emotions" (1990: ii–iii). Looking at this era from yet another perspective, Kay Young argues that the Depression was a crucial factor in the creation of the romantic comedy couple as equals, given the battering of masculinity by forces beyond its control. By "softening" the man and "defining" the woman in these films, "the Depression reinvented the couple to be the site for expressing rage/passion and for redefining the self in relation to the self's partner" (1994: 261). This chapter explores the multiple historical and cultural contexts, including the influence of immigrant director Frank Capra, across which the romance of the film is played out, especially those of class conflict and political ideology, thorny issues in an era of economic failure.

The stock market crash in October 1929 signaled the beginning of an American economic decline that lasted for a decade. Its rippling effects contributed to a financial collapse in Europe in 1931 and led eventually to a worldwide depression. The crisis in the United States occurred at the very moment when prosperity and a new consumer ethic were at their height in the 1920s. But the prosperity was built on shaky financial structures and practices. The great bull market of the late 1920s enabled easy profits because stocks could be bought on margin, with the buyer paying only part of the price and using the stock as collateral to borrow the rest of the money. Meanwhile, corporate mergers had concentrated wealth and financial control into the top 200 corporations, which represented 49 percent of all corporate earnings in 1929. If confidence failed in those businesses, declining stocks could bring down the entire economy. During the prosperous 1920s, the beneficiaries of these corporate earnings remained at the top; the gap between the wealthy and the poor widened dramatically because productivity increased far more quickly than wages. In 1929, while 70 percent of the population made less than $2,500 per year, the top 0.1 percent made more than $100,000. So the celebrated affluence of the 1920s was highly uneven, while new credit practices for cars and household commodities (buy now, pay later) encouraged debt and contributed to a saturated credit market. Eventually, the economy became dependent on the luxury spending of a wealthy minority at the same time as American exports fell off. In the mean time, the majority of Americans had become more vulnerable to the fragility of this vulnerable economy as populations shifted from farms to urban centers where workers were more likely to be affected by industrial lay-offs (McElvaine, 1993: 37–46).

The collapse of the economy was felt by the entire population, although urban workers fared worst while some at the top remained relatively unscathed. Between 1929 and 1933, unemployment rose from 3 percent to 30 percent, and among African Americans the percentage was much higher – up to 75 percent in some cities. Workers fortunate enough to keep their jobs faced reduced wages, so that by 1933 overall American income was 54 percent of what it had been in 1929 (Kyving, 2002: 209–21). Most historians point to the winter of 1932–3 as the lowest ebb of the Depression. Fifteen million people were unemployed, farm prices and factory production continued to fall, construction slowed, and multiple bank failures prompted governors in 38 states to institute "bank holidays," immobilizing the banking systems to prevent massive withdrawals.

The winter of 1932–3 was also marked by the uncertainties of the interregnum between Hoover and the president-elect, Franklin D. Roosevelt, who came to office in March 1933. Hoover was widely derided for pro-business policies that had failed to prevent the economic crash, but – in the wake of the 1917 Russian Revolution and "red" scares of the 1920s – Roosevelt was feared for his belief in a strong federal government which would centralize the American economy. As it turned out, Roosevelt's "New Deal" policies, adopted in the famous Hundred Days Congress immediately after his inauguration, were widely welcomed as first steps toward economic recovery. The founding of the Federal Deposit Insurance Corporation, for example, stopped bank panic by guaranteeing money in customers' accounts up to a certain amount, and the Agricultural Adjustment Act (AAA) controlled crop production to protect farmers from falling market prices. Suspicions and criticism of Roosevelt continued, and some of the reforms were later declared unconstitutional. Nevertheless, by the time *It Happened One Night* was being written and shot late in 1933, the worst of the Depression was over, even though full recovery was not yet in sight and the suffering continued, especially in the cities, where industrial employment was still low and mortgage defaults high. Until the end of the decade, every urban center had its own "Hooverville," a makeshift community of shacks for the homeless and displaced.

Hoovervilles, cultural displacement, and rootlessness are represented in *It Happened One Night* in the morning scene at Dyke's Auto Camp. When Ellie goes off to the communal showers and bathroom facilities, a tracking shot follows her as she passes through the grounds. This is the first time we see the auto camp by daylight: a series of clean but bare-bones cabins and, further in the background, more ramshackle outlying buildings that signal a run-down area. The families and children she passes on her walk do not look like tourists. Some carry buckets. Several are working on the grounds, raking and cleaning little plots of lawn around an occasional wheelbarrow. Harvey points out that although the auto camp provides overnight rentals, this scene clearly shows that some families live here: the women in line for the showers seem "at home" because these temporary quarters are indeed their homes. "We don't get the feeling that people like this have left their homes so much as that they make them, or find them, on the road" (1987: 113).

The *mise en scène* of most of the film is, as Harvey describes it, "consistently, conscientiously shabby ... with that anonymous washed-out look that only very familiar things acquire" (1987: 114) – oilcloth tablecloths, natty bathrobes, patched suitcases, the grey crowds milling quietly at bus stations, a country store with homemade signs. Despite the opening and closing scenes in the elegant milieu of the Andrews family, most of the film focuses on working-class and lower-middle-class life on the back roads in hard times. A group of hobos waves from a boxcar. A thief steals Ellie's suitcase at a bus stop; another thief steals Peter's bag after giving the couple a lift in his car. A gas station attendant is willing to trade gas for a hat. One of the film's contemporary newspaper reviews recognized this non-glamorous familiarity and praised its "honest documentation of familiar American actualities" (Troy, 1934: 427). In short, *It Happened One Night* takes great pains to specify its time and place as Depression-era America, where millionaires still sail their yachts but many more people ride the bus and use their last dollars to buy the tickets.

Americans were also still buying tickets to the movies, and *It Happened One Night* gives a nod to this in the scene of Ellie's big society wedding at the end of the film. Two shots linger on camera crews working large motion-picture cameras, obviously capturing footage that will be used in the newsreels that regularly accompanied feature films in theaters. Parts of the wedding scene are in fact shot in newsreel style, as Harvey points outs, "with poorly framed, asymmetrically composed long-shots photographed past intervening objects" (1987: 244). This is Capra's self-reference to movies, which remained the predominant popular entertainment during the Depression despite suffering setbacks earlier on. In 1929 and 1930, the novelty of talking pictures was still strong enough to buffer American cinema from hard times, but in the following two years, the industry suffered serious losses as audiences shrank and four of the seven major studios went into deficit. Almost one-third of neighborhood theaters closed. However, as Andrew Bergman points out in his history of Hollywood filmmaking in this era, even when audiences declined almost 25 percent during the worst of the Depression, they never entirely disappeared "and included a great many people who could scarcely afford to be there" (1971: xi).

To attract customers, theaters offered double features and began gimmicks like raffles and free crockery for ladies' matinees. They also lowered admission tickets from 30 to 20 cents, which was roughly the cost of two loaves of bread. At the same time, the sensational movies of the early 1930s – the sex comedies and violent gangster flicks – showed the "crassest expediency" of studios desperate "for whatever forms of shock or titillation would lure audiences into theaters as economic conditions worsened" (Sklar, 1975: 176).[1]

Ironically, Depression-era Hollywood sparkled with fluffy musicals, dazzling rhinestone costumes, and elegant high-society farces. Glamour became even more important to the economically strapped studios because contracts with fashion and cosmetic companies brought in extra income. "Tie-ins" to commodities ranging from Helena Rubinstein cosmetics to Buicks had begun in the 1920s but became even more widespread (Eckert, [1978] 1990: 107–8). Woody Allen's *The Purple Rose of Cairo* (1985) reflects the dynamics of glamour on-screen during the Depression: a housewife struggles to make do with her underemployed husband's meager wages while wholly losing herself at the movies, enraptured by Ginger Rogers' floating boas and beaded gowns. Most Hollywood films "tried to pretend the Great Depression did not exist": in 1931 a Motion Picture Producers and Distributors of America officer proclaimed that Americans "want light romances. No stark realism" (Doherty, 1999: 44).

Yet many films not only acknowledged the Depression but delivered stark realism and more. Fear found expression in the newly developed horror genre, while social anxieties found their way into the gangster film. Fallen-women films usually emphasized the grim economic reality that left women few choices. Even the glitzy musical *Gold Diggers of 1933* (1933) launches its story with a theater closing down, and in *Footlight Parade* (1933) an out-of-work producer laments, "Breadline, I hear you calling." Tellingly, glamorous stars Joan Crawford and Greta Garbo had slipped in box office popularity by 1933, overtaken by comic celebrities like Will Rogers, Marie Dressler, Eddie Cantor, Wallace Beery, and girl-next-door Janet Gaynor (Bergman, 1971: 4–71; Sklar, 1975: 178–81). Maltby finds these star ratings indicative of a crisis of masculinity: the lack of dashing romantic male leads reflects "the failures of the patriarchal hero" during the early Depression years, making the (new) Clark Gable persona of *It Happened One Night* especially appealing (1998: 141).

The Runaway Heiress

Considering these trends in early 1930s Hollywood films, it is less surprising that *It Happened One Night* acknowledges the Depression so directly, but the film also opens on a yacht and features an heiress as the romantic heroine. Far more interesting is how class issues play out in the film, with its portrayal of the wealthy Andrews family and the middle-class journalist who marries into it. Film historians see *It Happened One Night* as marking the beginning of a new way of portraying class in 1930s comedy. In the screwball genre begun by the film, wealthy people were seen as goofy but essentially good-hearted, which shows "how funny and lovable and harmless the rich could be" (Sklar, 1975: 188). Sklar argues that these films are wholly conservative, reaffirming that the social order needs no change, as proved by charming affluent romantics played by Cary Grant, Katherine Hepburn, and Irene Dunne (188). Yet these films undermine the social order in other ways. Molly Haskell sees the world of romantic comedies as one in which "male authority, or sexual imperialism, is reduced or in abeyance, while the feminine spirit is either dominant or equal" ([1974] 1987: 131). The question, then, is how class complicates the gender controversies of *It Happened One Night*, especially in light of its wealthy heroine.

As the character most removed from the majority of Depression-era spectators and also from the other characters populating the movie, heiress Ellie Andrews is a problem. How does she gain and hold our sympathy? She is introduced, approvingly, as the plucky daughter standing up to her bullying father. The narrative then quickly matches her to Peter as her equal in stubborn resistance to authority, so they become the couple whose romance we root for. But Ellie's carelessness, sense of privilege, and superficial values in the following scenes demonstrate that she needs to become a more deserving heroine. The low point is perhaps her eagerness to offer Peter money as a pay-off for not contacting her father. Peter's scornful reproach, calling her "the spoiled brat of a rich father," is the film's reproach as well. The first walls of Jericho scene, as chapter 2 showed, substantially changes Ellie's status in the story from the object of class scorn and sexual jokes to a sexually serious subject, and it ends with romantic backlighting to foreground Ellie as a traditional romantic leading lady. Her class conflict with Peter now urgently needs to be reconciled.

So the morning sequence at Dyke's Auto Camp, with its focus on Ellie, moves toward this reconciliation and also exemplifies the slippery nature of the gender–class dynamic. The first scene begins with a clever visual metaphor that distances her from her upper-class family. Ellie is shown waking to the buzz of a plane overhead, presumably the private plane in which we had glimpsed Mr. Andrews searching for her in the previous scene. In the relationship between these two scenes and the two shots, her father flies far overhead, while Ellie is located below, among the common folk at the auto camp. The shot composition of Ellie in the bed includes the open window behind her, through which we can see a man busy with a rake. Also, most of this scene is framed to show the entire room in broad daylight, baldly revealing the humbleness of the accommodation. In the moonlight the previous night, the room had been romantic, but daylight exposes its threadbare furnishings: an oilcloth on the table, a tin coffeepot on the stove, curtains that look frayed even from a distance.

Despite the low-class surroundings, Ellie's attitude has changed considerably from the night before. She stretches with a self-satisfied smile as she realizes where she is, and is genuinely pleased and grateful for Peter's gift of a toothbrush. She also thanks him happily for getting her clothes pressed, asking him where he had it "done" without seeming to realize that he has done the ironing himself. Peter is busy preparing breakfast, and though his manner is gruff to the point of sharpness, this is a reversal of gender roles, or a "softening" of the man's role, as Young (1994) puts it, which lays the foundation for the romantic comedy couple. The gender inversion is important in this scene, which registers class difference, given how the struggle for equality in 1930s romantic comedy involves – and, as Rowe (1995) suggests, perhaps conflates – gender and class.

The class difference is expressed in Ellie's surprise to learn that the "showers and things" are out on the grounds. "Outside?" she asks incredulously. Peter assures her that "all the best homes have them outside." But instead of pretension or outrage, Ellie mainly shows confusion about getting to the "things" wearing only her borrowed pajamas. Peter gives her his bathrobe and slippers to make this little trip, which is also a trip into a different world for Ellie. Richard A. Blake points out that Ellie has been borrowing Peter's clothes since she met him – his sweater and scarf on the bus, his trenchcoat in the rain, and, when she "crosses the border" in this morning scene, she is "completely covered in his clothes … wearing nothing of her own which would symbolically tie her to the past" (1991: 121). Wearing Peter's clothes is also part of the gender reversal in this scene. Curiously, the borrowed clothes on Ellie spark Peter's attraction toward her. For the first time in the scene, he smiles and, helping her into the robe, remarks approvingly about how "little" she is and how much he likes her hair unkempt. One reading of this is that Ellie is safely fetishized here, a "little" figure with uncombed hair, hardly resembling the heiress whose lingerie had dangled on the walls of Jericho the night before. Ellie is less threatening – both sexually and socially – in this gender/class masquerade as an auto-camp inhabitant heading to the outdoor bathroom.

Yet Ellie immediately demonstrates that she is still handicapped by the blinders of class. She sees the women outside the shower and even speaks to them, but she fails to see them as a *line* of women waiting their turn and so goes directly inside, where we hear the shouted protest of the shower user. The women in line hoot with laughter as Ellie realizes her mistake. "If you want to shower around here, you stand in line," one of them scolds. In the world outside the Andrewses' milieu, people stand in lines, even for showers. For the 1934 audience, the connotation would have been breadlines and employment lines, other common occurrences that Ellie Andrews would not, of course, "see." Ellie joining the back of the line is a comeuppance that would have had wider resonance as a rebuke to the wealthy few who were spared the lines for jobs or food during the Depression.

Embarrassed, Ellie meekly takes her place at the end of the line. A young girl in pigtails, delighted with an uppity woman being put in her place, sticks out her tongue at Ellie to make a face. Ellie quickly and gamely sticks out her tongue in return, a comic moment suggesting how far she has come from her introductory scene, when she was the cool brunette in her lounging gown on the yacht. But Ellie gives a small smile, too, as she settles into her place in the line, perhaps enjoying the novelty of common life, the life of "a plumber's daughter," as she describes it to Peter in the following scene.

The smile is a prickly issue. On the one hand, it shows Ellie learning to be a good sport, giving up pretentious airs, happily joining the auto-camp crowd. This is her border crossing (to use Blake's term), her transgression of the class line necessary for her union with Peter. On the other hand, her smile could be interpreted as a sign of privilege. As an heiress on a road adventure, her experience of Dyke's Auto Camp is very different from that of the residents who are "at home" there. For Ellie, this is an adventure. Spending the night in a risqué situation, in borrowed men's pajamas, has ended up being fun instead of dangerous. Is she enjoying this because she's slumming it?

The question is to what extent this scene can be counted as moving toward Ellie's embrace of humane and egalitarian values. As a scene about identification and empathy, its primary marking is gender – the line to the women's shower and bathroom. The implication is that Ellie's coming to consciousness as a woman – her growing desire for Peter – is imbricated in her consciousness of class. Yet there is no mistaking the class difference in this shower scene. The women in line are distinctly non-Hollywood types. The older ones are matronly, their fleshy faces set in perpetual scowls. The younger one is thin and colorless. Even in her oversized bathrobe, Ellie stands out, petite and shapely, her lipsticked mouth forming a perfect bow, her plucked eyebrows and eye-shadow attractively framing her face. So in this scene, which suggests Ellie's identification with women of other classes, she is pictured as both special and ordinary, which is a function of Depression-era narratives about the heiress. This is the key to understanding how it was possible for an audience in 1934 to connect with a heroine of such considerable wealth.

Both "Night Bus" and *It Happened One Night* use the runaway-heiress-in-the-headlines plot borrowed from 1930s celebrity gossip. The film version in particular punctuates the journey with close-ups of newspapers featuring Ellie's photo and glaring two-inch headlines: "ELLEN ANDREWS ESCAPES FATHER," "DAUGHTER OF ANDREWS STILL MISSING," and later, "ANDREWS WITHDRAWS OBJECTION." The real-life heiress in the headlines at that time was Barbara Hutton, who had inherited nearly $42 million from her grandfather, Frank W. Woolworth, founder of the Woolworth department-store chain. Barbara's father, Franklyn Hutton, was the cofounder of E.F. Hutton and Company, an investment firm which weathered the Depression particularly well. In 1930, Barbara's New York debut on her eighteenth birthday included a $60,000 ball at which 1,000 guests drank 2,000 bottles of champagne. Tabloid coverage of Barbara emphasized her profligate spending – $98,000 one afternoon at Cartier's in 1931 – which took on scandalous proportions as the economy grew bleaker for almost everyone else. Barbara was not the only one in her family prone to excess. The opening shot of a luxury yacht in *It Happened One Night* may well have been a reference to *The Sea Cloud*, the famous 350-foot yacht owned by Barbara's aunt, Marjorie Post Hutton. *The Sea Cloud* could sleep 280 people; it featured both a ballroom and a movie projection room. It was docked near the opulent Hutton estate in Palm Beach, Florida, which was the second largest private residence in the United States (after William Randolph Hearst's San Simeon). Both Marjorie and Barbara Hutton owned private railroad cars for luxurious trips between Florida and New York. Ellie's traversing of this route by Greyhound bus in the film is an ironic reference to Barbara Hutton's usual mode of transportation for this trip; the private railroad car cost $125,000 and included a bedroom suite, three baths, a dining salon, and an observation deck (Van Rensselaer, 1979: 81–4; Heymann, 1983: 30, 46, 48–9, 52–3).

Barbara Hutton also had a reputation as a poor little rich girl, and the press was as likely to highlight her miseries as her money. Her mother had committed suicide, and the 6-year-old Barbara was the one who discovered the body. Her father virtually abandoned her to relatives during her childhood and frequently expressed his displeasure with her behavior as an adult. The phrase "poor little rich girl" had become popularized by Noel Coward's 1925 song of that title, which satirized the flapper whose "love affairs are in a hopeless tangle" and whose life is "a wild typhoon." In 1931, Bing Crosby released the Harry Warren song "I Found a Million Dollar Baby (in a Five and Ten Cent Store)," which was an even more direct allusion to the Woolworth heiress, suggesting how strong an icon Hutton had become in popular culture.

In 1932, Barbara fell in love with "Prince" Alexis Mdivani, one of many displaced Russians claiming royalty in Europe at the time. Alexis and his siblings were known as "the marrying Mdivanis" for their skill in negotiating financially advantageous marriages; one of the brothers married the Hollywood star Pola Negri. Alexis was, in fact, married when Barbara became involved with him, and the press reveled in their illicit intercontinental romance. Barbara's father was deeply suspicious of his daughter's suitor, and rumors grew that Franklyn Hutton was himself the source of lurid scoops about the heiress and the playboy. After Mdivani was divorced, he married Barbara at a sumptuous and highly publicized celebration in Paris in June 1933. "Night Bus," published two months later, probably alludes to the playboy prince by giving its heiress a boyfriend named "King." But

It Happened One Night pushes the allusion much further. In the short story, King Westley never actually appears, but in the film he is played by British actor Jameson Thomas, whose striking resemblance to the wiry, foppish Mdivani could not be missed. In *It Happened One Night*, both Mr. Andrews and Peter call Westley a "fake" or "phoney," which is how the tabloids labeled Mdivani, whom they saw as an idle would-be aristocrat anxious to take advantage of the Hutton fortune.[2]

The heiress as poor little rich girl showed up often in Hollywood cinema during this era and no doubt contributes to the positioning of Ellie in *It Happened One Night*.[3] The characterization of Ellie as both privileged and misunderstood is developed in the scene in the cabin after she returns from the women's shower. Joining Peter in the breakfast he has prepared, Ellie describes her sheltered life of "nurses, governesses, chaperones, even bodyguards." She admits that Peter probably thinks she's "a fool and a spoiled brat," but she argues that she can't possibly be spoiled. "People who are spoiled are accustomed to having their own way," she says. "I never have. On the contrary, I've always been told what to do, how to do it, and when, and with whom." This part of their conversation is shot in one long take, with the camera focused full-frontal on Ellie's face, alight with expression as she explains her perspective. Peter is framed in profile on the left, slightly out of focus, his face skeptical as he listens to her story and responds with brief, smart aleck remarks. So the shot composition sets up Ellie's story sympathetically at the same time as it shows Peter barely listening. When her narrative segues into the story of how she met King Westley, Peter grows more irritated and initiates the topic of doughnut-dunking. The famous dunking exchange is a comic bit about class – her "finishing school" method of dunking versus Peter's supposed expertise. "Twenty million and you don't know how to dunk," he says in disgust. This can be read as one of Ellie's lessons in ordinary living (as discussed in chapter 1), but critics have also commented on the odd defensiveness of Peter's position here and the possibility that he is threatened by Ellie's exuberant willingness to change. Peter certainly fails to see the irony that his rigid rules about dunking are hardly different from other rules imposed on Ellie. She is

Peter uses doughnut-dunking as a pretext for lecturing Ellie on the faults of the upper class. Courtesy of Photofest.

once again being "told what to do, how to do it" – thus the cheerful mockery of her response, "Thanks, Professor." One possible reading, then, is that Ellie's foray to the women's shower signals a boundary crossing that Peter is still unwilling to make.

In the tradition of comic bad timing in romantic comedy, Peter's awakening and journey occur much later and too late. Not until the second motel scene, when Ellie crosses over to his side of the blanket wall, does he realize how much he has underestimated her. But his trip to New York, where he can gain the money and position to be a proper suitor, takes too long. In a cruel, class-based severance of the lovers, Peter's jalopy is passed by the convoy of Andrews family limousines. Then the separation is signified by a flurry of newspapers flying from the presses, with yet another flood of headlines: "ELLEN ANDREWS RETURNS HOME," "'GLAD TO BE HOME,' SAYS ELLEN," and, with the most bitter resonance for

Peter, "LOVE TRIUMPHANT." In the newspaper photos, Ellie looks coolly past the camera with the resigned unhappiness of the poor little rich girl.

Capra and Class Politics

The class-conflict romance of *It Happened One Night* was originally read as "a response to the Depression" which "cemented social classes": this kind of comedy "worked to pull things together" claims Bergman (1971: 133–4). In his influential work on Hollywood genres, Thomas Schatz similarly characterizes *It Happened One Night* as a fable showing that "the working-class stiff and the spoiled heiress can overcome their ideological disparity"; their union suggests "we should not lose faith in the traditional American ideal of a classless utopian society" (1981: 152). Sklar's interpretation, likewise, emphasizes the film as "a fantasy of upward social mobility" in which "The rich girl gives up her freedom for the hero, the poor boy weds his vitality and vision to the dominant social class" (1975: 207).

The huge box office success of *It Happened One Night* reflects the viability of these observations about utopian class fantasy during the Depression. However, later scholarship has offered other ideas as to how class operates in this film. Rowe, for instance, argues that this and other romantic comedies demonstrate "a displacement of class issues onto gender," using the romantic union to promulgate "the U.S. ideology that class doesn't matter." The heiress figure contributes to this displacement, and class becomes a marker of her unruliness rather than a real economic issue (Rowe, 1995: 118). Other critics have focused on how *It Happened One Night* idealizes not a "classless utopian society" so much as solid middle-class values. The character of Peter, for example, is no "working class stiff" even though he doesn't have a dollar to his name during the last part of the journey. Revising his earlier assessment, Sklar argues that, as a newspaper reporter, Peter is "a middle-class 'college man'" (1998: 45). More importantly, Peter is no "poor boy" in outlook and ideology. As Maltby puts it, his "middle-class virtues have to do with not accepting or expecting charity, living within your means, and not taking something for nothing," all "bourgeois virtues of dealing with money" which endear him to Mr. Andrews (1998: 155).

Charles J. Maland believes that the primary cultural work of *It Happened One Night* – its importance in the circulation of mainstream values and ideology – is precisely its affirmation of middle-class values during the Depression, when the ideology of hard work and individualism was most under siege. In this and the films Capra made in the following years, middle-class virtue is portrayed as vigorous and attractive. *It Happened One Night* achieves this vitality through Peter Warne, "a middle-class representative" who is "both a romantic hero and a moral spokesman who converts the heroine to his perspective" (Maland, 1995: 84, 180). Ellie's "conversion" is her renunciation of the aristocratic King Westley – a cultural fantasy of Barbara Hutton casting aside Alexis Mdivani and taking up with a reporter in the crowd.

The triumph of Peter Warne over King Westley became a signature move for Capra and promoted his reputation as a "populist" director, champion of the common folk and adversary of the powerful. The characterization of this Capraesque philosophy as a political belief was articulated in a widely cited essay by Jeffrey Richards ([1970] 1976). Richards traces Capra's ideology to nineteenth-century populist movements protesting the growing role of central government. For Richards, *It Happened One Night* is part of a growing political stand most explicitly expressed in the trilogy *Mr. Smith Goes to Washington* (1939), *Meet John Doe* (1941), and *State of the Union* (1948). For him, these films encapsulated middle-class dismay with the big-government policies of Franklin D. Roosevelt's New Deal, which were implicitly at odds with the American belief in self-help. For populists, economic problems began and ended with individuals, not "society." The more compassionate side of this philosophy was "good neighbourliness … if friends rallied round and people loved and helped one another, everything could be solved without government interference" ([1970] 1976: 67).[4]

In the "mythology" of populism, according to Richards, the most heroic figure is Abraham Lincoln, who is mentioned by Peter in

It Happened One Night. When Peter carries Ellie over his shoulder across a stream, Ellie is delighted with what she calls a "piggyback" ride. Peter once again uses this as an opportunity to contrast her uppity background with the lives of "real" people, who know that an over-the-shoulder ride is not "piggyback." "I never knew a rich man yet who could piggyback-ride," he says impatiently. "You show me a good piggybacker and I'll show you a real human. Now you take Abraham Lincoln, for instance, a natural-born piggybacker." The piggyback ride "epitomizes the simple, homely pleasures," unknown to people caught up in the "Big Business–Money Rat Race" (Richards, [1970] 1976: 68).

The problem with this political interpretation of *It Happened One Night* is that neither its "common folk" nor its wealthy aristocrats neatly fit the paradigm. The populist concept of "good neighborliness," for instance, is difficult to find. The sing-along scene on the bus seems to picture a populist ideal of "the simple, homely pleasures," and the scene is often cited as evidence of Capraesque warmth. Solidarity is suggested by the array of people here, including a man with the large beard of an Orthodox Jew, the effeminate sailor discussed in chapter 2, and a swarthy-skinned solo singer who might be of Italian origin. Yet, as Richard A. Blake points out, the illusion of good-neighbor solidarity does not hold up when a woman faints of hunger just a few moments later. No one moves to offer her food or take up a collection. In fact, most of the people Ellie and Peter encounter on the road demonstrate the desperation of "Depression-hardened America," where Shapeley hopes to extort reward money from Peter, thieves steal suitcases, and motel-owners don't hesitate to turn out an abandoned woman in the middle of the night (Blake, 1991: 123).

Even more problematic for populist politics is the representation of the upper class. The most obvious emblem of the Big Business–Money Rat Race is Mr. Andrews, who is transformed from bullying patriarch to loving father, and from obstacle to enabler of the romance and happy ending. The film continues to pit the down-and-out reporter against big money, but it is King Westley, not Mr. Andrews, who serves as a symbol of the self-indulgent rich. Critics often point out that Westley's publicity stunt arrival at his wedding in an autogyro (a one-man helicopter) betrays his egotism and superficiality. Later we learn that, just as Mr. Andrews had predicted, Westley can indeed be bought off "with a pot of gold," when he accepts $100,000 for an uncontested annulment of the marriage to Ellie. The substitution of Westley for Mr. Andrews conveniently allows for Peter's smooth transition into the Andrews family. But it also suggests the inconsistency of the film's "populism." Westley's autogyro may be a decadent toy, but is it really less decadent than Mr. Andrews' enormous yacht or the private plane in which we see him searching for Ellie? And Westley can be bought for $100,000 because Mr. Andrews can easily afford the pay-off, to facilitate Ellie's marriage to Peter.

Scholars have agreed that Capra's populist ideology is far less rigid than Richards implies, although resistance to big government is a salient theme in his later films (Levine, 1985: 187–92). However, contradictions about wealth such as those in *It Happened One Night* are characteristic of Capra's work. As Kendall puts it, "Capra's feelings about rich people were complicated, intense, and not particularly clear to himself," his "fierce populist streak" countered by his deep attraction to "safety, luxury, and power" (1990: 24). Analyzing these contradictions about wealth and power in Capra's films, Giuliana Muscio argues that Capra tended "to personalize conflict and to internalize the faults of society, searching for the origins of evil not within the system, but within the individual" (1998: 184). So big money is corrupt in *It Happened One Night* when we see Mr. Andrews as a grumpy autocrat on his yacht and Ellie as the privileged young woman who thinks buses wait for special passengers. But once the narrative reveals Mr. Andrews as a wise, doting father and Ellie as a woman who gives her last dollar to a hungry boy, the problem shifts from wealth to wealthy individuals, who may or may not be sympathetic. Further exploring Capra's popularity during the Depression, Muscio points out that his "neopopulism" was actually attuned to, not opposed to, the rhetoric of the New Deal, which "made an effort to transform itself into a sort of federalism with a humanitarian face" (1998: 183). She sees Roosevelt and Capra as being very similar in their appeals to solidarity and pragmatism and as highly appealing Depression-era figures who embodied different kinds of success stories: Roosevelt the patrician who overcame the obstacles of polio to become president, and Capra the immigrant kid who grew up to be "the name above the title" of successful Hollywood films (1998: 177).[5]

As we have seen, discussion of the class politics of *It Happened One Night* often involves Capra's outlook and beliefs and is usually linked to his impoverished background as an Italian Catholic immigrant. Capra's reputation as an auteur – that is, a director whose vision dominates his work – has been challenged because of his extensive collaborations (see introduction). Later, in the 1990s, there was a resurgence of critical interest in Capra as scholars reworked definitions of auteurs as "neither solitary geniuses nor sly transgressors" but artists "working out their ideas and visual styles in an industrial mode of production" (Sklar & Zagarrio, 1998a: 2–3). Examining how an artistic imagination emerges from specific historical conditions, Capra scholars have been particularly interested in his outsider status in conjunction with his film projects that champion the underdog and satirize or disparage Wasp culture.

Frank Capra was born Francesco Capra in Sicily in 1897. His family emigrated to the United States and settled in Los Angeles when he was 5 years old. In his autobiography, Capra represents himself as determined to transcend his "peasant" family through education but, because he "belonged to the riff-raff of Dagos, Shines, Cholos, and Japs," he was sent to the Manual Arts secondary school instead of Los Angeles High (1971: 6). His biographer McBride points out the implications of the racial associations: "With his dark complexion, wavy black hair, thick facial features, cheap clothing, and lack of social graces, Capra indeed appeared to be in the same category as a black or a Mexican" (1992: 53).

This categorization had wider resonance in the early decades of the twentieth century in the United States, given prejudice against dark-skinned Italians as an inferior "race," and the belief (supported by "scientific" evidence) that darker southern Italians were related to Africans and hence inferior to the more "Aryan" Italians of the north. Although Italian immigrants were in the long run able to benefit from their whiteness, they also suffered discrimination and criminalization as a "mongrel" threat to the nation (Guglielmo, 2003: 33–41).

Frank Capra winning the Academy Award for Best Director for *It Happened One Night*. He was known in Hollywood as "the little Wop." Courtesy of Photofest.

The racialized vocabulary that sorted out the value of immigrants by genetic descent was part of the American nativist movement which promoted the idea of a white "American race" (that is, rooted in northern Europe) against the growing number of immigrants from southern and eastern Europe who were literally changing the face of the United States. The young Capra experienced the pain of this exclusionary thinking, and in 1920 he Americanized his first name to Frank and added an English-sounding middle name, Russell, in order to imitate Wasp names such as Franklin Delano Roosevelt and William Randolph Hearst. The new name "didn't smell of the ghetto," he said (McBride, 1992: 45).

According to McBride, Capra was haunted by insecurity throughout his life, despite his successes. Ray Carney points out that Capra was "too short and swarthy to blend into the woodwork in a Hollywood of

Wasp – or Waspish looking – writers and actors" (1992: 39). The ethnic
distinction is also noted by Sklar, who quotes a 1935 *Collier's* article
announcing: "when anyone in Hollywood says 'The Little Wop,' anyone
in Hollywood knows that that means Frank Capra. And nobody's
offended, even the Italians. Certainly Capra isn't." As Sklar points out,
even though it is impossible to know who in fact was "offended" by
this language, the article shows how casually popular journalism in the
1930s used racist terminology "during an era when such markers mattered a very great deal" (1998: 46–7). According to McBride, during
the filming of *It Happened One Night*, Clark Gable casually used the
derogatory term too: " 'You know, I think this wop's got something,' he
remarked to Colbert about two weeks into the shooting" (1992: 307).

It Happened One Night is dotted with ethnic-looking faces in the
sing-along scene, and two African Americans appear briefly in the uniforms of bus-terminal personnel. Overall, the occasional presence of
the black servant or employee and the "whiteness" of the film was typical of 1930s studio productions.[6] The counting of black or ethnic
faces does not adequately address how whiteness is represented as the
Wasp culture that is disparaged but not altogether rejected in this film.
Describing this ambivalence about wealth and power in Capra, Carney
claims that, as the dark, ethnic outsider in Hollywood, Capra attained
"a creative critical perspective on the system of power" and "imaginative leverage" within structures with which he was never entirely com-
fortable (1996: 39–40).

In *It Happened One Night*, this "imaginative leverage" is particularly
notable in Peter's final scene, his confrontation with Mr. Andrews at
the palatial Andrews estate. This confrontation scene also suggests
what may have interested Capra in the short story "Night Bus," with its
cross-class romance leading to its genteel hero, self-described as financially "broke," facing down the "glare" of the formidable Mr. Andrews
in his spacious Wall Street office (Adams, [1933] 1979: 85–7). The
Capra–Riskin adaptation borrows a good deal of Adams's dialogue as
well as the plot turn: Mr. Andrews thinks Peter wants the $10,000
reward, is impressed that he actually wants only his expenses reimbursed, and gets him to admit his love for Ellie. However, the film
version sets the scene at the Andrews mansion on the day of Ellie's

wedding to King Westley. Thus, while we had previously seen Peter only in the milieu of the bus and back roads, he is suddenly positioned as the interloper at a society event he scornfully characterizes as a "three ring circus." The film also adds an encounter between Peter and Ellie that increases the class obstacles between them. More importantly, the film version makes Mr. Andrews a more sympathetic character and far more significant in engineering Ellie's union with Peter. Unlike the short story, which portrays Mr. Andrews as grumpy and disagreeable in this scene, the film takes great pains to show Mr. Andrews making a connection with Peter. The connection across the economic class lines involves middle-class values, and those values include a gendered agreement about women in relation to men's transactions and power.

The more affable characterization of Mr. Andrews is set up in the first scene of this sequence, when he finds his daughter in her room, depressed and weepy on her wedding day. This scene also alters the gender dynamics that make possible the shift in attitude toward class, because it shows Mr. Andrews acting from instinct and emotion. Mr. Andrews seeks out Ellie in her room because he senses that something is wrong. "I thought there was something on your mind," he says when she tearfully confides in him that she's in love with someone else. Mr. Andrews' position is entirely reversed from the opening scene, in which he was the oppressive tyrant. Now his primary concern is Ellie's happiness, even though he makes clear how he feels about King Westley. Father and daughter embrace, and she cries on his shoulder, apologizing for giving him a "scare" by running away. Backlighting of the two-shot imparts to their embrace a sentimental glow. Ellie confesses she has fallen in love with a man who "despises" her and who doesn't think very much of Mr. Andrews either, because he raised her "stupidly." Mr. Andrews is intrigued rather than offended by this description, and he pushes for an immediate meeting with Peter, working on a hunch that this mystery suitor is worthwhile. This new characterization of Mr. Andrews as the loving confidante calls to mind Kendall's comment on how Depression-era cinema engendered faith in "personality traits usually thought of as feminine – a moral subtlety, an unashamed belief in the validity of emotions" (1990: iii).

The other gender shift in this scene is Ellie's. No longer the impassioned woman who had breached the walls of Jericho, or the defiant daughter who had dived off the yacht, Ellie is in the more humble station of the woman rejected by the man she loves and resigned to a loveless marriage. She is also resigned to the constrictions of class status. Explaining why she can't possibly walk out on King Westley at this point, she says, "It would make us all look so ridiculous." Significantly, this passive Ellie is pictured in an upscale *mise en scène* in which her setting, dress, and behavior reveal even more privilege and luxury than we had seen on the yacht. For the first time, Ellie is pictured as movie-star glamorous. She wears a form-fitting satin wedding gown, the huge bedroom/sitting room is filled with cut flowers, and a maid appears to offer a tray of cocktails. When Mr. Andrews opens the door to seek her out, we find her smoking and lounging against plump silk pillows on a chaise lounge. This sumptuous bedroom is a startling contrast to the dumpy motel rooms she'd shared with Peter. Ironically, this fabulous room is the site of a greatly impoverished Ellie.

After she forces Mr. Andrews to produce the letter from Peter asking about "a financial matter," Ellie bitterly encourages her father to "pay him off." The sting of rejection was bad enough. Worse, Peter is now on the level of all the con men they'd met on the road. Money and class difference are suddenly as real and tangible as the divider blanket at Dyke's Auto Camp. Ellie believes her only option is immersion in class privilege. The scene ends with her embrace of King Westley. Desperate, she beseeches him to give her a life of "constant excitement" and never to let her get off the social "merry go round," a sad image of pointless spinning in comparison to her earlier journey of discovery. Maltby points out that Depression-era audiences would have recognized this "merry go round" as the excesses of the previous decade – "the stiff collars, cocktails, and stunts for the tabloid press of a circular and unproductive existence" (1998: 155). Ellie's regression to poor little rich girl threatens to end the more dynamic life and relationship she'd experienced with Peter. Certainly the embrace of status and class is a loss of sexual power. When she pulls back from Westley's kiss, we realize she is giving up the passion and eroticism she'd discovered in herself and which the film has associated with the back roads far from this Long Island estate.

Peter enters this class-charged scenario as the angry, righteous outsider who has been cheated – "taken for a buggy ride," as he tells Mr. Andrews, continuing the film's multiple images and metaphors of movement and travel. In "Night Bus," Peter and Elspeth are separated, but there is no misunderstanding that leads Peter to think he's been betrayed, so in this scene in the short story he is firm about wanting his expenses reimbursed, while Mr. Andrews shouts impatiently and blusters about his daughter. It would be easy, then, to read a Capraesque motivation into the film adaptation, in which the underdog Peter does the cranky shouting in a display of persistence and principle that wins the approval of the powers that be.

Peter's grouchy underdog role is played with comic effect, but he never loses his dignity. The scene begins with a focus on Peter, who is being shown into Mr. Andrews' study, the shot framed from behind the latter's desk to suggest his perspective on this stranger who "despises" Ellie and whom Ellie loves. Peter's face and demeanor suggest he is neither impressed nor intimidated by his surroundings – the ceiling-high bookshelves, the wainscoting, the servant who shows him in. But the itemized list Peter gives Mr. Andrews is a comical contrast to the highbrow setting. Peter has listed his cash output as $8.60 plus the cost of the items he traded for gas: topcoat, hat, suitcase, three shirts – altogether $39.60. "I sold some shorts and socks, too," he adds irritably, "I'm throwing those in." Reading the list, Mr. Andrews is given full-frontal framing at his desk, a symbol of authority similar to the desk at which Peter's editor was earlier seen. Mr. Andrews wears a formal morning suit in preparation for the imminent wedding. It's obvious that $39.60 would barely pay for his cravat. But Peter seems to know this, insisting that the sum is a "matter of principle." Having this modest amount reimbursed by Mr. Andrews means that he will at least not be cheated financially, even if he has been otherwise deceived. He does not want the $10,000 reward because that's not his due.

As Mr. Andrews begins to understand this, we see him repress a smile. The smile indicates his recognition of the values that will make

Peter an acceptable son-in-law, specifically "the bourgeois virtues of dealing with money," as Maltby puts it (1998: 156). Rowe notes the gendered implications of these values, which include those of "that most middle class of institutions, marriage": the transaction "seals Peter's alliance with Mr. Andrews and the film's collapsing of class onto gender" (1995: 135). This exchange of money in a highly masculinized setting – Mr. Andrews' study, dominated by his desk – is structured as an ancient kinship ritual of the exchange of woman from father to husband.

It Happened One Night stages moments of thrilling female empowerment but also moments of highly conservative masculine re-entrenchment, as seen in this cash transaction, with its intimation of physical violence, between Peter and Mr. Andrews. When the latter concludes the transaction and then presses his question, "Tell me, do you love my daughter?", another level of male bonding ensues. As we saw in chapter 1, the film's underlying macho violence is suggested by Peter's rough assertion that "What she needs is a guy that would take a sock at her once a day whether she had it coming to her or not." Do we interpret this film as a movie about putting women in their place or about women diving and sprinting away from their places? It depends on how much store we set by this scene of male collusion about uppity women.

Given these contradictions and Capra's background, another question is the weight of Capra's anxieties about uppity Wasp culture in relation to his anxieties about uppity women. McBride reads Peter as a character projected through Capra's own self-perception: Peter "is too insecure about his class status to believe that a woman from Ellie's background could love him" (1992: 306). In the confrontation scene with Mr. Andrews, the male bonding is qualified by Peter's insistence, till the very end of the scene, on the failures and defects of the Andrews family milieu. He tells Mr. Andrews exactly what he thinks of King Westley ("the pill of the century") and the entire swanky estate: "this joint … gives me the jitters." Peter is also blunt in his assessment of Ellie as an ingrate who takes things for granted and would drive any man "nutty," and of Mr. Andrews himself. Continually on the offensive, he accuses Mr. Andrews of not being willing to give him what he deserves, of not understanding "principles," and of failing as a parent in not giving Ellie "a sock" everyday: "If you had half the brain you're supposed to have, you'd have done it yourself." There is no denying a macho agreement about handling women here, but it's an agreement made without Peter giving ground on his critique of the Waspy triumvirate of Ellie, her father, and her legal husband.

Another question about this scene is how – or if – its machismo is mitigated by its comedy and its emotional pitch. Behind all the blustering and shouting, the real topic is love, and despite the macho posturing, the real question at hand is Peter's feelings. Masculine and forceful as Peter may be in this exchange, he is also a bit goofy in the tradition of Shakespeare's romantic-comic heroes – windy Benedick forced to admit he's sucker-punched by love. In Adams's story, Peter reveals he loves Elspeth in a speech made "in desperation" to Mr. Andrews (Adams, [1933] 1979: 87), but the film turns it into a funny line. "Yes!" Peter booms when he can no longer evade the question about whether or not he loves Ellie, "But don't hold that against me! I'm a little screwy myself!" Rowe reminds us that mockery of the male hero is made possible by the anti-authoritarian spirit of romantic comedy (1995: 102). This is the spirit in which the aggrieved underdog Peter strides into Mr. Andrews' empire demanding his $39.60. But the same spirit frames Peter's grand announcement of love, an emotion that makes him compelling and impassioned, but also a little screwy.

A sad coda about class distinctions follows Peter's furious exit from Mr. Andrews' study. The shot catches him stepping outside the door, suddenly stopped cold and looking off-frame left, his face drained of fury and simply pained. Peter has stepped into the pre-wedding celebration, a room abuzz with happy guests sipping cocktails. The eyeline shot is of Ellie on a stairway landing, posed like a goddess on a pedestal and surrounded by men in tuxedos. Her pedestal positioning above Peter foregrounds his alienation. In the study, he had been righteous. Now he is simply rejected. Nor can he recognize, as the audience can, the forced joviality in Ellie's voice when she lifts a glass to make a toast. "Well, here's to the merry go round," she is saying to her admirers – again, a code for the life of sumptuous misery to which she has resigned herself.

When she notices Peter leaving her father's study, her face falls and she approaches him to ask if he got the money he was after. Their tart exchange, each of them sarcastically congratulating the other, is their last conversation in the film, and when Peter walks out, refusing to stay for the ceremony, it's the last we see of him. From outside the massive oak doors, we see them open and close for him as he strides angrily toward the camera and, as the doors close behind him, we can see Ellie on the other side, looking after him. The huge wooden doors are far more substantial and impregnable than the walls of Jericho. She thinks he's taken $10,000 from her father. He thinks she's chosen King Westley. The class and economic wedge between the lovers suddenly catapults the relationship back to its earliest stages of class-based suspicion and ill will.

Again in the tradition of Shakespearean romantic obstacles, Ellie refuses to listen to her father, who could give her the information to change all this. Instead, the film heads toward her second wedding to the wrong man, a serious reminder that class division is real, that wealthy people marry other wealthy people, and that heiresses make terrible mistakes, which are bound to leave them hungry for love.

Chapter 4

Stardom
Shirtless Gable, Classy Colbert

Cave Man and a Menace to Morals

The star legend most often associated with Clark Gable is his devastating effect on men's undershirt sales following the release of *It Happened One Night*. According to this widely circulated story, in the wake of Gable stripping off his shirt to reveal a bare chest in the first motel scene of the film, sales of undershirts dropped nationwide by 30 percent. Sales didn't recover until World War II, when undershirts were required under military uniforms and men became accustomed to wearing them again.[1]

As it turns out, the undershirt sales story is an urban legend. No evidence from the garment industry or from undergarment manufacturers indicates a decline in sales at the time and, even if the titillating scene influenced movie fans, it would still be unlikely that the trend would cut across the entire industry so dramatically as to have an impact on sales (Urban Legends, 2008). Because films do influence fashion styles and because both Gable and *It Happened One Night* were so popular in the mid-1930s, it's entirely possible that going without an undershirt was considered sexy for men because of the film and became a trend. But because it's impossible to tell, in photographs and films, if men are wearing undershirts beneath their shirts, cultural documentation of this fad is difficult to track. The sales legend probably grew out of the way in which this scene circulated in the lore about Gable's appeal and in the impact of this film on his career.

The undershirt sales story exemplifies how stardom works as a cultural production across multiple media – the films themselves, studio promotions, publicity, gossip, journalism, and consumer products. Arguing for an understanding of stardom as a multimedia construction, Richard Dyer claims that the star industry conceals its own manipulations. The popularity of stars is inherently ideological, he contends, relating to ideals of how people would like to imagine themselves. Yet because stars are real people, their very existence serves to "prove" the values they represent, so the manufacture of the star by the film industry and by the media is well disguised ([1979] 1998: 20–1). Clark Gable's stardom in the 1930s was tied to cultural ideals and contentions about masculinity, and he went on to become one of the great masculine icons of American cinema. He became known as an actor who always "played himself," who expressed his own rugged manliness without "acting" on-screen, a reputation that he shared with icons John Wayne and Gary Cooper. Calling them "natural actors," Dennis Bingham points out, amounts to calling them "natural men," a label that reflects their significance in popular understandings of gender (1994: 16, 220).

Drawing on the film theory of stars as "texts" that possess ideological currency, this chapter explores how the stardom of Clark Gable and Claudette Colbert was invoked and developed in *It Happened One Night* and how stardom in this film intersects with the subjects of gender, genre, sexuality, and class, which were discussed in the previous chapters. A retrospective on *It Happened One Night* in *The Nation* claims that, before the film's release, "neither Claudette Colbert nor Clark Gable was a reigning favorite with the great popular public" (Troy, 1940: 426). Both stars had a fan base, and Gable in particular had a reputation as a heart throb, but *It Happened One Night* was certainly the major turning point in their careers, winning them Academy Awards, prestige, and choice roles for years to come. In turn, their star personas were important factors in the development of the romantic comedy couple in cinema.

Of the film's two stars, Clark Gable (1901–60) is the one who made a long-term impact on popular culture, and his role in this film was pivotal. As Maria DiBattista puts it, "It was screwball comedy that rescued Gable from the psychopathology of his early roles – tough-talking

In his early years of stardom, Clark Gable was promoted at MGM as the woman-izing tough guy, an appealing figure of powerful masculinity during the Depression. Courtesy of Photofest.

gangsters whose sexual hold over dames ... doesn't last long once they get their fill of his rough-housing" (2001: 165). Born into a working-class family in Cadiz, Ohio, Gable began making a name in movies in 1930 after nearly a decade of on-and-off theatrical experience around the country and some bit roles in silent cinema. To support himself between acting jobs, he also worked as a garage mechanic, a loader for a lumber company, and a lineman for a telephone company. His six-foot-one frame and dark good looks attracted the attention of film-makers who typecast him as a heavy, noting his resemblance to the popular boxer Jack Dempsey. Playing villains, he attracted the interest of MGM executive Irving Thalberg, who decided to put him under contract and groom him as a star because MGM badly needed a sexy male romantic lead for the new talkies era.

More than that, Depression-era culture was ready for a high-profile masculine ideal. At a time when many American men could not feed their families, the most widespread image of masculinity was the forlorn figure of "the forgotten man," the laborer betrayed by the corporate world.[2] The crisis of capitalism was a gender crisis. Remember the hungry mother and son in the bus scene in *It Happened One Night*, with the mother promised a job in New York and no father on the scene at all. Writing about the creation of the Clark Gable myth, Joe Fisher emphasizes how the Depression was understood as a defrauding of "authentic" American men by "effete, European, Wall Street men, men no longer in touch with the land and lacking the ability to tame and control it" (1993: 38). In short, it was the prime cultural moment for a macho star associated with working-class values and sexual power.

An MGM publicist recalled that Gable was "the personification of the old American expression 'he-man,' so all we had to do was build on that" (Harris, 2002: 69). The "building" by the studio involved tutoring, promotion, and physical improvement. To amplify Gable's image as a rugged outdoors type, experts were called in to enhance his shooting and fishing skills. His physical makeover included body-building, new eyebrows, and a new hairstyle. His press biography glossed over the fact that he had spent most of his pre-Hollywood time in theatre and instead characterized him as an adventurer and oil wildcatter (Harris, 2002: 70). Anxious to cash in on their investment, MGM put Gable through a blitz of quick films. In 1931, 12 films were released featuring Gable in fifth to top billing. To guarantee high visibility, he was paired with top box office draws Joan Crawford, Norma Shearer, Greta Garbo, and Jean Harlow in melodramas and crime films. Many of the former were "women's films" which were built around the stardom of the female lead, but they also garnered a female audience for Gable.[3]

The early studio profile for Gable was sexy but not romantic. An MGM staff memo from this era described the prototype Gable character: "He's tough, uneducated, got a hell of a temper, can fight his weight in wildcats … with sex that drives the woman crazy" (Fisher, 1993: 37). The language of fan magazines continued the discourse of raw sexual power. An article in *Modern Screen* in 1932 spoke of his "magnetism" and "bad boy appeal." "His love making is not romantic, it has not 'glamor,' it is of the earth, earthy" (Baldwin, 1986: 48). A *Photoplay* essay, also from 1932, praises him as "the epitome of the ruthless, handsome, knock-'em-down, treat-'em-rough, virile, modern cave man" (quoted in Connelly, 2004: 39). Clearly the "cave man" appeal for women trumped sentimentality during this part of his career.

Early 1930s movies often glamorized the gangster hero who was successful in his illegitimate access to money and power – an especially appealing character during the Depression. So it is not surprising that Gable was frequently cast as a sexy underworld character. He played gangsters or gangster associates in *Dance, Fools, Dance* (1931), *A Free Soul* (1931), and *The Finger Points* (1931). He also played a would-be murderer in *Night Nurse* (1931) and a con man in both *No Man of Her Own* (1932) and *Hold Your Man* (1933). His identification with the figure of the hoodlum associated him with violence toward women, the flip side of the adulated "cave man" persona. The best-known image from *The Public Enemy* (1931) was James Cagney hitting Mae Clarke in the face with a grapefruit over breakfast, an iconic scene which established the gangster's contempt for and control over women – another manifestation of the crisis of masculinity during the Depression. Gable's tough-guy star image suggested a similar kind of violent control over women. The *Modern Screen* article praising his earthy appeal (see above) claimed that, while Gable "might adore the current heroine to the point of madness," he might also "give her a very good beating – and get away with it" (Baldwin, 1986: 46). Two of his early films play this out. In *Night Nurse* the Gable character plans to murder the heroine and at one point punches her unconscious. In *A Free Soul*, he shoves Norma Shearer into a chair and says, "Sit down and take it and like it. You're an idiot, a spoiled, silly brat that needs a hairbrush now and then." As Fisher puts it, "Gable's actual and threatened violence became, at least for MGM executives, an 'acceptable' objective correlative for sex" (1993: 37). The threat of violence in *It Happened One Night* can be seen as a continuation of this aspect of Gable's stardom. It is a dimension of Peter's character that is not present in "Night Bus." The tough talk about Ellie needing "a sock" would have been, for 1934 audiences, a manifestation of Gable's "he-man" persona.

MGM's construction of this persona and the pairing with top-ranking female sex symbols paid off. Beginning in 1932, Gable was consistently ranked in the top ten box-office stars, a ranking he maintained until 1942. Writing of Gable's quick rise in Hollywood, a 1932 *Screenland* article by Ben Maddox reported that "The Gable craze can be likened only to the Valentino boom of yester-year" (1970: 21). The "craze" was fueled by Gable's reputation as a womanizer whose pursuit of the leading lady did not end on the screen. Studio publicity made much of his marriage to Maria (Ria) Langham, which ended in 1939, but gossip columns hinted pointedly at his torrid relationships with Joan Crawford and Jean Harlow, among others.

MGM profited from Gable's reputation as an off-screen Don Juan. The gushing Maddox article coyly asks if fame is threatening Gable's marriage, triumphantly asserts that it won't break up, and ends with an ambiguous acclamation of his appeal: "To the women he's brought a new brand of love," encompassing both women in the audience and the women in his private life (1970: 174). However, in an era when Hollywood morals were being attacked by powerful church and social groups, stars had a "moral turpitude" clause in their contracts which gave studios the power to dictate the details of their stars' private lives. In 1931 Gable and Crawford were individually summoned to Louis B. Mayer's office and told that if their relationship didn't end, they would lose their jobs (Spicer, 2002: 83).

As protests against immoral conduct in movies and in Hollywood society mounted, Gable was a frequent target. In addition to the rumors about his private life, his films often flaunted the themes of adultery, prostitution, and pregnancy out of wedlock. In *Red Dust* (1932), one of his most successful films, he plays a rubber-plantation owner dallying with the wife (Mary Astor) of one of his employees and then falling for a prostitute on the run (Jean Harlow). In its most talked-about scene, he has a suggestive conversation with Harlow while she bathes in a rain barrel into which he gazes with frank approval before grabbing her by the hair and dunking her into it. The "kept woman" film *Possessed* and the bootlegger drama *Dance, Fool, Dance* provoked heated conflicts between MGM and the Hays Office. Father Daniel Lord, SJ, who had contributed to the formulation of the 1930 Code and continued to be an influential voice in Hays Office politics, called Gable "a menace to morals" and condemned *No Man of Her Own* as a "filthy" movie that "violated every possible article" of the Production Code (Maltby, 1998: 146; Spicer, 2002: 96). Given the pressure for censorship, MGM began to rethink its promotion of the sexually aggressive image of Gable. MGM's loan of Gable to Columbia later that year for *It Happened One Night* allowed MGM to make a small profit on Gable, who was between film projects, and allowed the much smaller Columbia to use an A-list star. For MGM, the added benefit was seeing how Gable performed in an entirely different genre; it was a safe way to experiment with his persona further without taking a financial risk (Maltby, 1998: 146–8).

Gable was not Capra's first choice for the film. For the part of Peter, Capra and Riskin wanted Robert Montgomery, an MGM romantic lead who had acted in fluffy comedies like *Our Blushing Brides* (1930) and *Blondie of the Follies* (1932). When Montgomery turned them down and MGM gave them Gable instead, Capra claims he was "a little disappointed" because Montgomery, unlike Gable, could do comedy (Friedman, [1960] 2004: 51). Gable himself admitted in later interviews that, when he read the script, he was uncertain about his ability to play the comic bits (Spicer, 2002: 105). But as it turned out, Gable's switch of genre, from crime drama and melodrama to comedy, freed him from narrow typecasting and opened up his career. In turn, the gender reversals and goofy antics of romantic comedy gave him the opportunity to introduce a new kind of romantic hero, grumpy but tender, willing to make breakfast, iron a dress, join a sing-along, and declare that he's a little screwy.

The casting also lent the new genre of romantic comedy the spark of sexual electricity. For audiences of 1934, the suggestiveness of the walls of Jericho scene was no doubt enhanced by watching Gable the fabled womanizer – hinted at in his teasing song about the big bad wolf – playing a far more restrained character, who quietly asks Ellie to remove her underclothes from the blanket divider. Besides staring at Harlow naked in a rain barrel, Gable had walked in on Carole Lombard while she was taking a shower in *No Man of Her Own*. So his respect for this far more chaste heroine, Ellie Andrews, would have added to the sexual tension of this scene for fans who relished the bad-boy sexuality of the Gable persona.

"Who Do You Think You Are? Clark Gable?"

In key moments of *It Happened One Night*, Gable brings to the character of Peter some of the tough-guy grittiness from his MGM image but he also shows that he is able to mock it or play against it. In the scene outside the bus with Shapeley, for example, Peter quickly morphs into a callous gangster bragging that his boss, "Killer," is hoping for "a million smackers" for "that dame." It is another of his quick improvisations, like the one devised for the detectives at Dyke's Auto Camp. This time, Shapeley – the smarmy salesman who had attempted to make a pass at Ellie – had shown Peter the newspaper photo of Ellie and demanded half the reward, $5,000, threatening to expose her otherwise. Peter quickly takes Shapeley aside and "admits" he's kidnapped Ellie for far more money than the $10,000 reward. He tells Shapeley that he has machine guns in his suitcase because there's likely to be a shoot-out further up the road. When Shapeley panics and babbles that he's a married man with kids, Peter grabs his lapels and threatens his family, warning him to think about a family man who talked too much and "blew his brains out" when he found out what happened to his kid.

But this gruesome threat is buffered by its set-up of Peter play-acting here, the reporter pretending to be a gangster. For Gable fans, the play-acting would have been especially clever as a reference to the characters he usually portrayed.[4] The conversation with Shapeley is filmed as a medium two-shot with backlighting, Shapeley mostly in shadow but the moonlight silhouetting Peter's profile as he leans in menacingly toward the terrified salesman. This shadowy glamorization of the thug is a nod to the era's gangster genre, but the scene ends in comedy. Scrambling to get away, Shapeley gets a running start and falls flat on his face before he races into the distance. Peter, meanwhile, who had pointed his finger in his pocket to threaten Shapeley with his "gun," spits on the ground in a stereotypical good-riddance gesture of the mobster. But in a comic coda, he does a double take and quickly brushes his jacket shoulder before turning back toward the bus: the would-be gangster had spit on himself.

The scene that most parodies masculinity, however, is the hitchhiking scene, part of a road sequence that ends with Peter stealing a car. This sequence also demonstrates the inflection of Gable's image in *It Happened One Night*: the effectiveness of his playing against type, the comic mockery of his own macho persona, and his ability to bring that persona to bear in the latter part of the sequence.

Along with the walls of Jericho scene, the hitchhiking scene is legendary in movie history, emblematic of the power struggle in romantic comedy and its eccentric protagonists. This scene follows the night in the hayfield, so the attraction between Peter and Ellie has been acknowledged, but now in broad daylight they are coping with two practical problems. They have no transportation and no money for breakfast. Limping down the road in her high heels, Ellie insists they stop and rest on a fence until some cars show up so they can start hitchhiking. The topic of food and hunger immediately launches them into a bickering conversation about class. Peter whittles and munches on his raw carrot, castigating her for turning it down. "I forgot – the idea of offering a raw carrot to an Andrews," he says scornfully, adding, "Hey, you don't think I'm goin' around panhandling for you, do ya?" The panhandling reference is important because it is tied here to class issues, while at the end of this sequence it becomes tied to gender.

But both class and gender are embroiled in the ensuing conversation, which in turn draws on and satirizes Gable's screen persona of down-to-earth masculinity. Peter brashly proclaims himself an authority on hitchhiking. In fact, he plans to write a book about it, he boasts, called "The Hitchhiker's Hail." Ellie settles herself on the fence and feigns interest in yet another lecture. Peter's previous lessons and lectures have been about doughnut-dunking and piggyback riding, homely arts which he has interpreted as triumphs of the common folk over the out-of-touch wealthy classes. Hitchhiking is an even more class-sensitive topic, given the Andrews family's use of yachts and private planes for transportation.

For Peter, hitchhiking is also a specifically masculine art. "It's all in the thumb," he explains with a swagger, brandishing his raised thumb in its erect mode. Still whittling and munching his carrot, he proceeds to demonstrate, with flamboyance, each of his three expert hitchhiking hails, while Ellie leans forward on the fence to interject dubious and mocking commentary, the tone of which he fails to notice. The comedy of this exchange lies in the timing of their banter and the contrast between Peter's goofy demonstrations of his hails and Ellie's wry responses, caught in one long take in a medium shot that links them as a couple connected by humorous conflict: male arrogance and female skepticism. "Keep your eye on this thumb, baby, and see what happens," Peter announces as he rushes out to the road to put his lecture into practice, thumb up and ready to work its magic.

The results are predictably humbling. When his first expert hail gets no results, Peter is left staring at his thumb in bewilderment. "Still looking at that thumb," Ellie calls from the fence. As a dozen more cars shoot by without stopping, Peter gets more and more desperate in his hailing techniques, finally resorting to the flailing gestures he'd spoken of disparagingly as "amateur." The shot is framed from across the road, so the speeding cars whizz between Peter and the camera, while Ellie lounges on the fence in the background, grinning. Finally, Peter thumbs his nose at the final car, a gesture the Hays Office decided was "not offensive" (Maltby, 1998: 136), and walks dejectedly back to the smiling Ellie, hat in hand, utterly but comically defeated. The puncturing of male egotism is funny, but especially pungent is its enactment by Gable, the "cave man" idol engaging in floundering, harebrained physical comedy.

The humiliation continues when Ellie tells him she's going to stop a car for them. Peter laughs at her and then is stunned and alarmed to see her raise her skirt, as if to adjust her garters, at the side of the road. A car comes by, and close-ups show a classic cheesecake shot of Ellie's legs, then a man's foot in the car hitting the brakes and a hand wrenching the clutch. Arguably, it's a cheap laugh. Sikov complains about the sexist implications of the disembodied leg and the joke's implication

Topping Peter's self-proclaimed authority on the subject, Ellie shows Peter that she knows how to stop a car. Courtesy of Photofest.

that a "woman who can succeed on her own is reduced to a posed leg, a moving hand, and a piece of skirt" (1989: 90). But the sexist leg shot is Peter's comeuppance for his sexist cockiness, raising the stakes on the sexual tension. As Harvey points out, it's also Peter's comeuppance for his haranguing lectures on how to dunk doughnuts and give a piggyback ride: "He is teaching the heroine to be ordinary," and she shocks him by doing "something large and outrageous," suggesting that "she is unconventional and he is not." Besides, "He may know a lot, but she knows what stops traffic" (1987: 117).

A wipe cuts to the next scene of a sulking Peter and beaming Ellie as passengers in the back of the car. Indignant that Ellie has used sex appeal when his male cleverness had failed, Peter sarcastically asks if she would "take off all her clothes" to get more cars to stop. Ellie is unremittingly cheerful in her replies, and the driver, hearing them squabble, assumes they're newlyweds and begins to regale them with an improvised song about love. The sheer awfulness of his song becomes a rallying point for Peter and Ellie, and soon they are whispering and suppressing their laughter in the backseat, naughty conspirators, masquerading once again as a married couple.

The tone quickly shifts when the driver stops to get himself some lunch and asks if anyone wants to join him. Peter gruffly interrupts Ellie, who had started to accept his invitation.[5] "We're not hungry," Peter says sullenly. Still stinging from his hitchhiking humiliation, Peter is now further humiliated by the powerlessness that must have struck a deep chord for Depression-era audiences: Ellie is hungry, and he has no way to provide for the woman he loves. A medium shot frames the three of them in the car, with Peter turned away from the other two so that the camera can see, as they cannot, the pain on his face. Peter's hat is pulled low on his forehead so his eyes are in shadow, literalizing his shame. When the driver goes into the country store for food, a tight two-shot on Peter and Ellie shows their tense conversation. Peter accuses Ellie of planning to "gold-dig" the driver for food, and she admits that was her intention. "Gold-digging" was a buzz word in the 1920s and 1930s for female trading of sexual favors for money, wryly celebrated in a film like *Gold Diggers of 1933*. Peter's use of the word raises the stakes on this disagreement, which is as much about gender as about food.

Ellie pushes her complaint. "No fooling, I'm hungry," she says, and Peter angrily digs around in his coat pockets for a carrot. Clearly, this is a question of male pride. Ellie is willing to use her feminine wiles for food. But all Peter can produce is a raw carrot, ironically pathetic as a phallic symbol in this scene. Kendall points out the sharp contrast with Gable's former gangster/con man/plantation-owner characters: Peter Warne "has no pretenses to social power. He's broke; he's out of a job; he can't even run fast enough to catch the guy who stole Ellie's suitcase [in an early scene at a bus rest stop]. He's a surprisingly frank embodiment of the ineffectuality of the American male in the face of the Depression" (1990: 45).

In what follows, Peter's shame erupts into a threat of violence. Ellie refuses the carrot (suggesting emotional and sexual refusal, as discussed in chapter 1), and begins to go into the store after the driver.

Furious, Peter delivers a harsh rebuke straight from his repertoire of rough-house thugs. He grabs her forearm and snarls, "You do and I'll break your neck." As we saw earlier, this is part of the undercurrent of male violence toward women that haunts the film and which enables the interpretation of It Happened One Night as a conservative restoration of male power over women. But its effect here is embarrassment. A shocked silence follows the outburst. For Peter, the eruption has exposed his shame about being unable to provide for her. For Ellie, the possessiveness of the gesture, in conjunction with Peter's prudish reaction to her lifted skirt, is a reflection of the patriarchal control she'd dived away from at the beginning of the film. They quietly walk away from the car to a bench on the lawn, where Peter shyly takes Ellie's hand and apologizes. The tenderness of his gesture and tone of voice plays against Gable's persona in the same way as the comedy of his disastrous hitchhiking.

Significantly, the narrative pulls back from this gentle moment and gives Peter the opportunity to reassume his masculine power. His apology is interrupted when the driver sneaks out of the store, jumps into his car, and drives away with Peter's suitcase. Peter runs after him down the road, and a wipe shows the passage of time and Peter's return with the car and suitcase but without the driver. Peter is rumpled, hatless, and sporting a cut on his cheekbone. He got the car, he said, by giving the thief a black eye and tying him to a tree, an event that sounds both exaggerated and somewhat innocent, like the report of a schoolyard brawl. The significance of this is the contrast to Peter's earlier pursuit of the thief who stole Ellie's bag at the side of the bus. This later chase is successful even though more improbable (in its suggestion of Peter's ability to outrun a car), but it redeems Peter from his lowest point in the film as an emasculated figure threatening violence against a woman to spare his pride. Instead, the violence is not only displaced onto someone else (who deserves it, in the world of macho fisticuffs) but displaced from the screen entirely, maintaining Peter's (and Gable's) cleaner romantic hero image while allowing him to act as masculine protector.

As Peter and Ellie drive away in the commandeered car, their relationship is summarized in a touching pantomime. In a medium two-shot, Ellie lovingly wipes the cut on Peter's face and quickly caresses his hair as she moves her hand away, a gesture so intimate that it makes Peter wince, clearly not from the pain of the bruise but from the bruising knowledge that she is another man's wife. He instructs her to empty his coat pockets so they can barter the coat for gas. Going through his coat, Ellie finds the bunch of carrots, and quietly begins to nibble on one. Seeing this, Peter's face is suffused with tenderness and pain. This is what he had so gleefully wished for two days before – the humbling of the heiress, and now he himself is humbled by it. He hadn't counted on loving her too much to want her to suffer.

That Gable's star image could encompass romantic comedy illustrates what Judith Mayne has identified as the malleability of stardom, its capacity for "constant reinvention, the dissolution of contraries, the embrace of wildly opposing terms" (1993: 138). Stardom, in turn, depends on concepts of individuality that enable fans to read a star "text" coherently despite its contradictions and changes over time. The apparatuses of stardom, from film close-ups to biographies, encourage the identification of a star's "coherent continuousness" which "becomes what the star 'really is'" (Dyer, [1986] 2004: 9–10). For Gable, the keynote of virile masculinity links the variety of acting styles he exhibits in *It Happened One Night* – the tenderness, comedy, and self-deprecation play off a baseline "Gable." This masculinity also connects him to the values of the American Everyman. In terms of the larger narrative spin on power, for instance, Peter's tussle with the road thief is a small victory on the road to his face-off with Mr. Andrews, which he wins through brute honesty, not brute force. For the Depression-era audience, he exhibits the vulnerability and frustration of male economic loss, but the narrative also allows him to recoup that loss by triumphing over the wealthy King Westley.

Fisher argues that Gable's star-persona masculinity is redefined in *It Happened One Night* as "an 'integrity' which cannot easily be overcome because it represents an independent and incorruptible manhood, big and strong enough to take on corporate America and win" (1993: 41). In short, Gable's iconic masculinity took on political and cultural significance, for the reasons discussed in chapter 3. Critic Alexander Walker situates him alongside other 1930s stars Gary Cooper, Henry

Fonda, and Jimmy Stewart, symbols of the male individualist who "could exert power to get things done," an icon that was badly needed as the nation struggled to recover its economy and status (1970: 298).

Because of this enhanced persona and because *It Happened One Night* was far more popular than any of his previous films, Gable's ranking at the box office went from number 7 to number 2 by the end of 1934 (just behind Shirley Temple, illustrating the appeal of family-friendly stars at this time). For the first time, Gable was the object of female fan hysteria. When MGM sent him on tour to promote his next film in 1934, he was mobbed by 2,500 women at a train station in Kansas City. Women wept and handed him articles of their clothing during his appearances in Baltimore, San Francisco, and New York (Williams, 1968: 45; Spicer, 2002: 107). Police motorcades escorted him to his film openings, and when he won the Academy Award for his role as Peter Warne, his salary at MGM doubled. The hat and raincoat he'd worn in the film and the little mustache he'd grown all became popular styles for men, and "Clark Gable" became short-hand for suave masculinity. Men "tried to imitate his brashness, his skepticism, his secret tenderness" (Jordan, 1973: 56). "Who do you think you are? Clark Gable?" became "an overnight catchphrase" for women putting down would-be dapper guys (Harris, 2002: 118–19). By the end of the decade, he was dubbed "The King," Hollywood's top romantic lead, a fitting nod to his first important victory in movies, where he had nudged aside an effete pretender.

Tough Dame, Lovely Frog

Claudette Colbert (1903–96) brought to *It Happened One Night* far less celebrity attention and cultural baggage than her co-star, but in return she brought more prestige, as indicated by her salary for the picture, $50,000, which was five times that of Gable's. Colbert ranked near the top of Paramount's leading ladies in the early 1930s, with a star image that appealed to women as "the chic, superconfident female" (Parish, 1972: 102). When she began filmmaking in 1929 she already had the gamine look that would become her signature: short bobbed hair, bouncy bangs, apple cheeks and huge, mischievous eyes.[6] Colbert's persona was elegant and sophisticated, but she was no diva like her Paramount colleague Marlene Dietrich, nor was she a sex siren like Joan Crawford or Mae West. Writing of her star image, DiBattista claims that despite Colbert's "European chic" presence, she "was utterly American in the modernity of her look and attitudes" (2001: 162).

Yet Colbert's classy star profile was partly a consequence of her European roots. Born Lily (Emilie) Chauchoin into a middle-class French family near Paris, she emigrated with them to the United States when she was a little girl. Lily grew up in a bilingual household in Manhattan and attended a city high school that encouraged dramatic arts. She had barely graduated when she began work on the stage, where she changed her name but insisted on a French pronunciation of the new surname, not Col-bert, but Col-baire. By the end of the decade, she was an up-and-coming Broadway star, but by then the talkies had made film the new media for serious actors, while Broadway was waning in its cultural importance. Colbert moved to cinema and signed a contract with Paramount, "the most Continental" of the major studios, headed by Austrian producer Adoph Zukor, who brought to his studio a reputation for stylish fare and upscale decor (Dick, 2008: 43–4).

Colbert made 20 films for Paramount between 1929 and her loan to Columbia for *It Happened One Night* at the end of 1933. She accrued consistently good reviews even when the films themselves were often lackluster, and her appeal to women is suggested by some of the heroines she portrayed during this time: a newspaper columnist whose success threatens her marriage in *Young Man of Manhattan* (1930); a saleswoman whose marriage to a widower is threatened by her less than blueblood background in *The Lady Lies* (1929); a quick-witted woman who is able to save her fiancé from a trumped-up murder charge in *The Wiser Sex* (1932). She also played a number of suffering, male-victimized heroines typical of the era's women's films. Film historian Jeanine Basinger points out how Colbert's character in *Torch Singer* (1933) taps into this stereotype when, impoverished, she is forced to abandon her child and take up a nightclub career. Told she needs to suffer to be a torch singer, Colbert cries, "Watch me suffer!" – a retort Basinger characterizes as "the key slogan of the early thirties woman's film" (1993: 399).

By then, Colbert was reportedly disgusted with Paramount where "there seemed to be nothing but a succession of dreary assembly-line roles and films ahead for her" (Parish, 1972: 100). What saved her box office profile was a sexy role as the seductive empress in Cecil B. DeMille's *The Sign of the Cross* (1932), a film that suddenly made her "the latest sex goddess of the screen," as biographer Quirck put it (1985: 52). *The Sign of the Cross* was a sensationalist take on Nero and early Christianity, with lush displays of Roman decadence and the cruel torture of scantily clad Christians, all of which enmeshed the film in controversy with the censors. Playing the wicked Empress Poppaea, Colbert is introduced bathing in a sunken pool of asses' milk which foamed suggestively around her naked breasts.

With its reputation as a shocker, *The Sign of the Cross* was a huge box office draw. "What mattered to Claudette," biographer Dick reports, "was not that DeMille had a hit … but that she had a role that moviegoers would remember" (2008: 69). This is significant: in 1933, the Hollywood choices for this gifted actress were watch-me-suffer melodramas and, for a larger audience, sex goddess extravaganzas. It is not simply that *It Happened One Night* opened up Colbert's career, but rather that it opened up a genre where the heroine can enjoy both the virtue of the melodramatic heroine and the sexuality of the siren.

Once Capra and Riskin had created this new heroine, the problem was casting. "Almost no female stars in Hollywood in 1933 called themselves comediennes," Kendall reminds us. Carole Lombard wasn't yet a big name and Irene Dunne hadn't yet done comedy. The few who had – Myrna Loy, Miriam Hopkins, Margaret Sullavan – turned down the part (1990: 38). Colbert, though not their first choice, had demonstrated she could play a heroine with both a light touch and depth of feeling. In Ernst Lubitsch's operetta *The Smiling Lieutenant* (1931) she was the savvy mistress who gamely teaches the wife how to be sexy in an outrageous musical number, "Jazz Up Your Lingerie." And in the satire *Three-Cornered Moon* (1933) she played a wealthy woman forced to join the workforce when the family fortune fails. The film's premise of "throw the rich into the refining fire of Depression America" may have been what gave Columbia pictures chief Harry Cohn the idea of pursuing her for *It Happened One Night* (Dick, 2008: 72–3).

In addition to her versatility, Colbert brought to the film her reputation as a sophisticated, independent, modern woman, an image evoked in part by her unusual marital arrangement. She had married Broadway co-star Norman Foster in 1927, but they never lived together and finally divorced in 1934. Dick explains that the arrangement was due to her formidable mother who "would not allow Norman to become one of the family," insisting that a "conventional marriage" would threaten Colbert's career (2008: 30). Colbert was entirely dominated by her mother, Dick explains, who even insisted on an abortion for her daughter at one point in order to preserve her screen image (249). The public explanation of the marriage arrangement was more romantic. According to the Quirck biography, Colbert insisted "they deliberately lived apart 'to keep our love alive'" (1985: 10). A *Modern Screen* article from 1931 quotes Colbert declaring that having an evening with Foster is "quite as exciting as if we were engaged," and describes her as a woman "who would fling traditions and conventions to the wind and live as she wanted to live" (Fletcher, [1931] 1986: 166). Nevertheless, some of the fan magazines more archly called Colbert a "Part-Time Wife" and Foster a "bachelor husband" (Dick, 2008: 30).

The innuendoes were obvious. Gable's biographer Warren G. Harris claims that, because of the star's notorious homophobia, Gable did not make a pass at Colbert as he usually did with his leading ladies, because he "knew that she was a lesbian in a sham marriage" (2002: 113). But to borrow the cautionary words of Mr. Andrews' steward, it's not as simple as all that. A *Vanity Fair* article quotes two sources who claim that Colbert told them she "went all the way" with Gable and could give anatomical details (Collins, 1998: 121). This article refutes a *National Enquirer* piece published just after Colbert's death which purported to out her as a lesbian and to expose an affair with Marlene Dietrich when they were both at Paramount in the 1930s. The Dietrich rumor had been around for decades, springing from a widely circulated photograph of Colbert seated in between Dietrich's famous legs on a "chute-the-chute" at a 1935 beach party. Though the rumor has never been corroborated by Dietrich's biographers, Colbert was included in Kenneth Anger's *Hollywood Babylon* tell-all as one of Dietrich's "good-time Charlenes who, like Marlene, swung both ways" (1975: 177).

The Dietrich story gained currency because of Colbert's curious history. After her divorce from Foster, she married a physician, Joel Pressman, and remained married to him until his death in 1967. However, they lived apart after the mid-1950s when she moved to New York and then the Caribbean. Through most of her life, she enjoyed the company of gay men in the arts, so she was often spotted in the social circles of Noel Coward, Bill Blass, George Cukor, and others. In the late 1950s and early 1960s, she and lesbian painter Verna Hull became "an item" in gossip columns. They lived in penthouses on the same floor in a building in New York and later in adjacent houses in Barbados (Dick, 2008: 253). In the last years of Colbert's life, she had similar arrangements with Saks Fifth Avenue executive Helen O'Hagan, who vigorously denied in interviews that Colbert had ever had a sexual relationship with a woman.[7]

Dick's biography spends an entire chapter backing O'Hagan's claim and rebutting "the spreading stain" of Colbert's lesbian reputation, which – according to O'Hagan – Colbert herself labeled "a stigma" (2008: 251, 253, 316 n. 251). The rumors, he said, had developed because her closest relationships were always with women, possibly as a result of the matriarchal household in which she was raised (254). William J. Mann, who includes Colbert in his history of gay and lesbian Hollywood, suggests that the rumors may show that rigid sexual definitions are not always useful. Colbert was "known for marching to a different drummer," he says, but for women of the 1930s romantic friendships were common and "sexual definitions were often more fluid and different from men" (2001: 83), a notion that queer theory posits more generally about sexual categories.[8]

These conflicting stories and histories about Colbert attest not only to the complications of sexual identification but also to conflicting cultural wishes, fantasies, and anxieties about stardom. The point is not the "truth" of Colbert's identity as lesbian, straight, or bisexual, but rather that the controversy strikingly illustrates popular assumptions about star identity. Richard DeCordova describes stardom as a system of revelations, "a logic of secrecy" which assumes that "real" identity involves the star's private life, so that sexuality – involving the most private behavior – is the most authentic and "the most truthful" core of identification.[9] We can see this logic at work in the *Vanity Fair* article, which piously refutes the Dietrich–Colbert story but uses the famous photo as its title illustration. Drawing on Foucault's concept of sexuality as a "secret" that is constantly being produced and deployed, DeCordova (1990) argues that stardom, with its emphasis on sex appeal, is itself a major factor in any era's production of sexuality. DeCordova glosses over the political implications of this production, but we can see in the arguments whirling around Colbert how competing claims are embedded in sexual politics and biases. The suspicious interpretation of Colbert's "modern marriage" tantalizingly offered the illusion of a "real" Colbert for certain fans and social circles, even if this kind of speculation took place below the radar of Colbert's mainstream stardom in 1933–4.

Given this controversy at the margins of her image, there is some irony in Colbert playing the role that was to influence representations of heterosexual romance until the end of the twentieth century and beyond. The romantic comedy film has become heterosexuality's most widely circulated story, and its protagonists its cultural ideals. While the male hero of this comedy is usually attractive by current standards – from Cary Grant in the 1930s to Hugh Grant at the end of the twentieth century – the hero can also be average-looking or plump or plain, as played by Tom Hanks, Jack Black, Dustin Hoffman, and Seth Rogen. The heroine, in contrast, is held to a much higher and less flexible standard of attractiveness, which includes not just physical attributes but ideals of race and class.[10]

Claudette Colbert plays the Wasp ideal with its specific meanings of both whiteness and upper-crust gentility. As Dick puts it, "Although Claudette did not come from Park Avenue, she did come from the avenue below it, Lexington, and knew the difference between them. She could also play the residents of either equally well" (2008: 84).

Claudette Colbert brought to the role of Ellie Andrews both prestige and a reputation as a sophisticated, independent modern woman. She also brought the WASP looks and demeanor that remain a standard for the romantic comedy heroine. Courtesy of Photofest.

DiBattista adds that Colbert's physique plays to class stereotypes too: her "high cheekbones and petite, elegant frame" connoting urbane and genteel origins (2001: 162).

Her French origin gave her additional upscale validation, as can be seen in Capra's description of his meeting to persuade her to accept the role of Ellie. His account of the visit he and Riskin made to her house has the comic tone of an American tall tale, but its humor is revealing too. Admitted by her maid, he claims a "big French poodle" bit him on the seat of his pants before Colbert could appear. "Froggy was in a French tizzy," he says, because she was packing for a vacation, and this made him realize she was "perfect for the part of the rich heiress: spoiled, bratty, lovely." Colbert agreed to take the role for double her usual salary at Paramount. "Claudette had a mind as bright as a dollar, and a French appreciation of its luster," Capra reports. Leaving with Riskin, he told him, "Tough dame, that lovely frog" (Capra, 1971: 165–6). As an immigrant from a country with far less glamorous connotations in 1933, Capra piles up the French stereotypes and uses the derogatory name with some irony and even affection, but it's also clear that he's pleased to have gotten a leading lady with a pedigree, poodle and all.

For 1930s audiences, the class meanings of Colbert's Frenchness found their material manifestation in contemporary haute couture. French styles "ruled fashion design" in the 1920s and 1930s, according to historian Lois Banner. The American garment industry followed Parisian clothing trends, and upscale department stores advertised their women's clothing as being "of the French mode" (Banner, 1983: 278). The idealization of the French as arbiters of upscale taste meant that, unlike immigrants (such as Capra) from Italy and southern Europe, the French never acquired the disrepute of being less than "white," no matter how swarthy their complexions might be – exemplifying a particular historical construction of whiteness. Colbert reinforced the upscale French fashion image with her reputation for her own personal clothing taste. For her films at Paramount, she insisted on using the costume designer who also designed her own personal wardrobe, and she preferred simple, modern styles for herself on-screen and off (Tapert, 1998: 177–8).

Colbert also plays Ellie with full-bodied sensuality. Harvey claims Capra was the first to find and use Colbert's combined "primness and tactility." "Colbert is one of those actresses who makes us feel her body, especially in the angle and set of her hips," he says, pointing out how she settles her backside into the bed at Dyke's Auto Camp and later settles it on the fence while Gable does his hitchhiking routine. On the first night of the bus, she begins the trip seated beside Gable leaning forward, "like a receptionist having a bad day," but ends up asleep against him, clutching his lapel. Later, when she is offering to pay him and "insisting on the distance between herself and the upstart newsman," she still places her hand on his chest and arm (1987: 113).

In addition, Colbert brought to the role the quickness and intelligence that would become vital for the romantic comedy heroine, including the verbal acuity that DiBattista values in the genre's "fast-talking dames," descendants of Shakespeare's resourceful comic heroines. Kendall points out that up until her Empress Poppaea debut in the sunken bath, "Colbert with her round face, wide smile, and mischievous eyes, was not considered a beauty; she was a wit" (1990: 39). Commenting on Colbert's star reputation along these lines, Tapert adds that "The sophistication and self-reliance she brought to her roles were native to her personality. And her wit was as quick as any dialogue ever written for her" (1998: 183). In *It Happened One Night*, Colbert's verbal fluency and quick thinking can be seen in Ellie's bristly interactions with her father and her first conflict with Peter about the seat on the bus. And at the beginning of the second motel scene, she displays the duplicity and guile of Shakespeare's Rosalind or Viola when she quietly hides the newspaper announcing that her father has forgiven her. As she talks Peter into spending one more night with her, we can watch her face struggling with both the dishonesty and the truth behind the dishonesty – her feelings for Peter and her panic about going back to Westley. As Rowe points out, *It Happened One Night* gives Ellie "a degree of subjectivity it doesn't give Peter, in long close-ups of her eyes which show her to be reflecting on the changes within herself and her feelings for Peter" (1995: 132).

The Runaway Bride

This subjectivity is apparent in the film's famous penultimate scene, the escape of the runaway bride, in which Colbert's performance is notable for its physical and facial expressiveness. Ellie doesn't say a word in the entire scene, which focuses on her reactions and what she might be thinking as she goes through the motions of a stately, formal, and sacrosanct ceremony. Again, the film favors Ellie rather than Peter by giving her the grand dramatic gesture that will wrap up the plot, but it also distances us enough from Ellie that there's some suspense about what exactly she will do, given her earlier comment that a change of mind would make the Andrews family look "ridiculous." The wedding scene is filmed in documentary style at first, with long shots emphasizing the depth and size of the wooded estate where the wedding guests gather and where King Westley's autogyro hovers and lands. A wipe takes us to the chamber orchestra striking up the first notes of the traditional Mendelssohn wedding march, and an angelic female choir chimes in, amplifying the dignity and sacredness of the ceremony. In the next montage, we see the procession of half a dozen groomsmen, the media men with their cameras rolling, the priest waiting at the altar, and finally the unsmiling bride and her father beginning their march down the aisle. In a final reminder of the solemnity of the occasion, a shot of the procession shows Ellie and her father as tiny figures in the rear of a line headed by the grooms-men who dominate the shot, a nod to the patriarchal framework of both marriage and the Andrews enterprise. The larger structure of this patriarchy is signified again when they arrive at the altar, and the shot of the bride and groom is taken from behind the crucifix. Church, state, and family are at stake in this ceremony, making its disruption all the more outrageous.

A medium two-shot frames Ellie and Mr. Andrews as they march toward the altar. Quietly and utterly at odds with the solemnity, the latter says in a low voice, "You're a sucker to go through with this." The audience understands, as even Mr. Andrews himself may not, that this will have an electric effect on Ellie because her father is using Peter's word. "Did anybody ever make a sucker out of you?" Peter had demanded in the previous scene with him. It's the word Peter had used with Ellie too, cajoling her to relax behind the walls of Jericho on the first night – "Don't be a sucker" – and again on the night in the moon-light, when he'd called himself a "prize sucker" for helping her. During his self-revealing monologue about his dream island and ideal woman, he called himself a "sucker" for hoping for such things. It's a slang word, tough and streetwise, that comes easily to Peter the hard-drinking journalist and is glaringly out of place during a wedding march outside a swank Long Island mansion.

If the word is a clue to Peter's return to her life, Ellie is careful not to betray it. The power of her performance in this scene is its convey-ance, through the tiniest flinches and glances, of emotions she dare not express. Through most of her father's low-pitched speech, she keeps her eyes carefully screen left as she walks with him, looking over at him only when he says, "That guy Warne is okay. He didn't want the reward. All he asked for was $39.60." When he tells her, in an even lower voice, "He loves you, Ellie. He told me so," she closes her eyes for a moment as the impact of it registers. But there is no evidence in her expression that she is going to take her father's advice. After all, her father has openly opposed her marriage to King Westley. Can she trust him now to encourage her desertion of Westley for an unemployed reporter?

The minister begins the ceremony by posing the traditional question about anyone coming forth with an objection, and Mr. Andrews visibly stifles a retort. The minister then asks the ritual question of Westley: "King, wilt thou have this woman …" to which Westley promptly gives the traditional assent. But when the question is posed to Ellie, we see her breath coming fast and her chest heaving in the low-cut gown. Her mouth and jaw twitch, but instead of speaking, she shakes her head passionately, turns around, and flees back down the aisle. A long shot catches her bounding across the lawn, the veil streaming behind her, pursued by the cameras and the shocked crowd. The film's last glimpse of her shows her safely in the getaway car, slamming the door on the voluminous train of her gown.

Kendall calls the escape "one of the most joyous, kinetic, and rebellious images produced by mass culture in the Depression" (1990: 49). But there is no agreement among the film's critics about the meanings and implications of this scene. Is this a woman claiming her happiness or obeying her father? The films begins with Ellie's rebellion against Mr. Andrews, and it ends with her doing exactly what he wants. "You can make an old man happy," he whispers to her as they march toward the altar, "and you won't do so bad for yourself." The narrative has turned back on itself so that making the old man happy makes the rebellious daughter happy, too. It redeems powerful fatherhood by recasting it along the axis of sentimentality and transforms the defiant daughter into the wholly conventional figure of the wife, illustrating the conservative nature of romantic comedy. Ellie refuses one wedding so she can choose another. Does it matter that one wedding is a Long Island bash and the other an elopement to the Michigan woods?

As Rowe puts it, "Peter and Ellie must be seen as capable of becoming Ward and June Cleaver" (1995: 135). Similarly, Maltby argues for the film's appeal as "a return to older, more ordered values" in which fathers know best (1998: 156).

Yet as film history attests, this image of a woman defying the establishment and the sanctity of her own wedding is powerfully iconic. The runaway bride appears again at the close of *The Graduate* (1967), a film which more seriously flouts the establishment and redeems neither fathers nor mothers. Its disrupted wedding scene uses the crucifix, Capra's understated symbol of authority, with far less respect. For an even later generation, the eponymous heroine of *Runaway Bride* (1999) is a serial jilter at the altar, a romantic heroine determined to resist marriage until she meets her match. The movie is a canny tribute not just to *It Happened One Night* but to all the unruly women of romantic comedy. Citing even more mutinous female unruliness, Peter N. Chumo claims *Thelma and Louise* (1991) as a dark version of *It Happened One Night*, its fugitives similarly eluding the authorities and improvising new identities, the outlaw Thelma its madcap runaway bride (1991–2: 23–4).

For Claudette Colbert, playing the original runaway bride was her own escape from dreary weepies and garish epics. Eight years later, while she was still at the top of her career, the wicked imagination of Preston Sturges positioned her as a bride once again at the opening and closing of *The Palm Beach Story* (1942) which reverses the route of *It Happened One Night*, taking the screwball couple – married and separated – from New York to Florida to find each other again and to remarry. *The Palm Beach Story* ends with a bold title shot posing the question romantic comedies shunt aside. "And they lived happily ever after … Or did they?" Colbert's stardom in both films is a witty link between Capra's optimism and Sturges' cynicism about romance and marriage. Hollywood keeps retelling *It Happened One Night* through romantic comedy because Sturges' question is so irksome and daunting. We want to give it a resounding "Yes!" but we know it's not as simple as all that.

Notes

Notes to Introduction

1 The other two films to make a sweep were *One Flew Over the Cuckoo's Nest* (1975) and *The Silence of the Lambs* (1991). The other comedies to win for Best Picture were *You Can't Take It With You* (1938), *Going My Way* (1944), *Tom Jones* (1963), *The Sting* (1973), and *Annie Hall* (1977).

Notes to Chapter 1

1 Hits of the past three decades include *Romancing the Stone* (1984), *Moonstruck* (1987), *When Harry Met Sally* (1989), *Pretty Woman* (1990), *Housesitter* (1992), *French Kiss*, (1995) *You've Got Mail* (1998)), *Notting Hill* (1999), and *My Big Fat Greek Wedding* (2002).

2 "Screwball" is a term used by scholars in a variety of ways, sometimes synonymously with "romantic comedy" (Neale & Krutnik, 1990), sometimes referring only to the cycle of the 1930s and 1940s (Sikov, 1989), but at other times with reference to a zany style of romantic comedy that continues today (Preston, 2000). For an overview of the various uses and meanings of the term, see Henderson (1986: 311–13) and Gehring (1986: 3–12). See also McDonald for the place of *It Happened One Night* in these discussions (2007: 18–26).

3 The "meet cute," which introduces the main characters in a funny, provocative, or unlikely situation, has been a favorite narrative device for scriptwriters since the 1930s. See McDonald (2007: 12).

4 Smoking had specifically been associated with "women's freedom" in a 1929 American Tobacco Company ad campaign (Landay, 1998: 89).

5   The joke about Ellie's backside is reprised in a later scene when Ellie leaves her bus seat to escape a large man sleeping beside her. The only empty seat is the one next to Peter, who promptly pretends he too is asleep, with his hand fallen on the seat beside him, palm up, waiting for her to sit on it.

6   Carney suggests that these gifts place them in the tradition of Huck Finn, Tom Sawyer, Daisy Miller, the Chaplin tramp, and Flem Snopes, the long line of versatile, trickster Americans figuring out identities as they move along (1996: 233).

Notes to Chapter 2

1   The entire text of the Production Code is included as an appendix in Doherty (1999: 347–68). It is also available at www.artsreformation.com/a001/hays-code.html.

2   See Pennington (2007: 8). For a detailed description of the development of the Production Code and the transition from the Hays Office to the Breen administration, see Leff and Simmons (1990: 3–54).

3   This scene is a precedent for the split-screen pillow talk between Doris Day and Rock Hudson in *Pillow Talk* (1959). Also, Shumway points out that the walls of Jericho screen is alluded to in *Desperately Seeking Susan* (1985) when Roberta and her would-be lover sleep in the same room with a flimsy division between them (2003: 104).

4   See also Leland Poague's comparison of Bergman (1971) and Cavell (1981) on the topic of the walls of Jericho (1994: 26–30).

Notes to Chapter 3

1   For details of how the film industry reacted to the Depression in terms of structure and economics, see Sklar (1975: 161–73).

2   For details of Barbara Hutton and the relationship with Mdivani, see Van Rensselaer (1979: 57–73, 91–103) and Heymann (1983: 57–76).

3   As Maria DiBattista explains, Depression-era movies were likely to portray the heiress "as an object of pity, captive to her own wealth ... Prey to fortune hunters and insulated from the bracing affections of the common folks, she is often portrayed as substantially poorer in the things that really give life its zest." DiBattista points out that this theme is played out in a film released later that year, *The Richest Girl in the World* (1934), about a wealthy young woman

impersonating her secretary in order to find a man who will love her for herself instead of her riches (2001: 90).

4   Drawing on a less politically explicit notion of populism, Gehring traces Capra's "populist legacy" through American film history, describing a "power-to-the-people genre" of which Capra is the "archetypal author" (1995: 2). He argues that the Capra tradition can be found in films through the 1940s and again in the populist revival beginning in the late 1970s, in films such as *The Electric Horseman* (1979) and *Dave* (1993) and in the work of auteurs such as Ron Howard who celebrate common folk up against big institutions.

5   See also Poague (1994) for a detailed analysis of the limitations of Richards's concept of populism. Drawing on Robin Wood, Poague claims that it might be more useful to emphasize how all ideologies are characterized by unresolvable contradictions that shape the dynamics of Hollywood genres (1994: 23–30).

6   For whiteness as a cultural construction developed in specific ways in classic Hollywood cinema, see Bernardi (1996, 2001) and Dyer (1997).

Notes to Chapter 4

1   This anecdote about Clark Gable's influence on men's fashion appears in several Gable biographies (Williams, 1968: 44; Harris, 2002: 118; Spicer, 2002: 109), in Colbert's biography (Quirck, 1985: 65), in fashion histories (Chenoune, 1993: 184), and also in scholarly film studies (Wood, 1975: 190; Young, 1994: 259). In 1995, the American Movie Channel reported it as part of a feature on Hollywood fashion fads (Gottschalk, 1995: C1).

2   Many of these unemployed laborers were also veterans of World War I, thousands of whom marched on Washington in 1932 as the self-named Bonus Army. The US Army was ordered to disperse them, and in the subsequent shooting two veterans were killed. This history is fictionalized in the 1933 film *Gabriel Over the White House*.

3   Timothy Connelly points out the importance of his roles in two "fallen women" films of the era, *Susan Lenox: Her Fall and Rise* (1931) and *Possessed* (1931), in which Gable plays a sympathetic love interest who has to lose or renounce the heroine. These two films emphasize the misery of Gable's character which parallels the misery of the heroine. In contrast to most of his work at this time, these films showed that Gable could offer "a version of masculinity that recognizes and shares in the suffering caused by sexual desire," hinting that his he-man gruffness hid a tender heart (Connelly, 2004: 38–9).

4 The scene may in fact be a subtle allusion to *The Finger Points* (1931), in which Gable plays a crooked reporter who gets involved in the gangster activity he is supposed to be covering.

5 Cavell points out that Ellie's interrupted reply continues the equation of food and love in this film. She is about to say, "That would be lovely," but instead says, "That would be love –" (1981: 92).

6 Tapert points out that Colbert did not alter her looks or persona throughout her 60-year career (1998: 167) and insisted on managing her own film image, from hairstyle to costumes (177).

7 See also O'Hagan's statements to the press in response to the *National Enquirer* publication, at which time she described Colbert as "a man's lady" who had been linked to stars such as Maurice Chevalier, Gary Cooper, and Fred MacMurray (Rush & Molloy, 1996: 14). The *Vanity Fair* article, however, claims Colbert was not involved with any man after her marriage to Pressman (Collins, 1998: 123).

8 Mann quotes Christopher Isherwood's lover Don Bachardy, who knew her as "Uncle Claude" and describes her as being in "a very closeted situation. Only well within her own circle did they know the truth" (2001: 82). But Mann also quotes William Haines, a friend of Colbert's, "well within her own circle," who claims he "never knew she was a dyke" (83).

9 This dynamic is evident in David Bret's (2007) biography of Clark Gable, which asserts that Gable's secret bisexuality early in his career is the key to "his story as it has never been told before" (as the cover blurb promises). Because Bret gives few sources and corroborations for his stories, his biography has not had the impact of the sustained and continual stories about Colbert, which have arisen from various sources in a more consistent way over the decades.

10 See my elaboration and analysis of this topic (Mizejewski, 2007).

Works Cited

Adams, Samuel Hopkins. [1933] 1979. "Night Bus." *Stories into Film*. Eds. William Kittredge and Steven M. Krauzer. New York: Harper Colophon.

Altman, Rick. 1999. *Film/Genre*. London: British Film Institute.

Anger, Kenneth. 1975. *Hollywood Babylon*. San Francisco: Straight Arrow.

Bailey, Beth. 1989. *From Front Porch to Backseat: Courtship in Twentieth-Century America*. Baltimore: Johns Hopkins University Press.

Bakhtin, Mikhail. [1965] 1984. *Rabelais and His World*. Trans. Hélène Iswolsky. Bloomington: Indiana University Press.

Baldwin, Faith. 1986. "Why All the Mystery about Gable's Appeal?" *The Best of Modern Screen*. Ed. Mark Bego. New York: St. Martin's, 46–8.

Banner, Lois. 1983. *American Beauty*. New York: Knopf.

Basinger, Jeanine. 1993. *A Woman's View: How Hollywood Spoke to Women, 1930–1960*. New York: Knopf.

Bergman, Andrew. 1971. *We're in the Money: Depression America and Its Films*. New York: Harper.

Bernardi, Daniel, ed. 1996. *The Birth of Whiteness: Race and the Emergence of U.S. Cinema*. New Brunswick, NJ: Rutgers University Press.

Bernardi, Daniel, ed. 2001. *Classic Hollywood, Classic Whiteness*. Minneapolis and London: University of Minnesota Press.

Bingham, Dennis. 1994. *Acting Male: Masculinities in the Films of James Stewart, Jack Nicholson, and Clint Eastwood*. New Brunswick, NJ: Rutgers University Press.

Blake, Richard A. 1991. *Screening America: Reflections on Five Classic Films*. New York and Mahwah, NJ: Paulist Press.

Boehnel, William. 1934. Review of *It Happened One Night*. *New York World Telegram* (February 23).

Bowman, Barbara. 1992. *Master Space: Film Images of Capra, Lubitsch, Sternberg, and Wyler*. New York, Westport, CT, and London: Greenwood.

Bret, David. 2007. *Clark Gable: Tormented Star*. New York: Carroll & Graf.

Buscombe, Edward. 1998. "Notes on Columbia Pictures Corporation, 1926–1941, with a New Afterword." In Sklar and Zagarrio 1998b, 255–81.

Capra, Frank. 1971. *The Name above the Title*. New York: Macmillan.

Carney, Ray. 1996. *American Vision: The Films of Frank Capra*. Hanover, NH and London: Wesleyan University Press.

Carson, Diane. 1994. "To Be Seen but Not Heard: The Awful Truth." *Multiple Voices in Feminist Film Criticism*. Eds. Diane Carson et al. Minneapolis and London: University of Minnesota Press, 213–25.

Cavell, Stanley. 1981. *Pursuits of Happiness: The Hollywood Comedy of Remarriage*. Cambridge, MA: Harvard University Press.

Chauncey, George. 1994. *Gay New York: Gender, Urban Culture, and the Making of the Gay Male World, 1890–1940*. New York: Basic Books.

Chenoune, Farid. 1993. *A History of Men's Fashion*. Trans. Deke Dusinberre. Paris: Flammarion.

Chumo, Peter N. 1991–2. "*Thelma and Louise* as Screwball Comedy." *Film Quarterly* 25.2 (Winter): 23–4.

Collins, Amy Fine. 1998. "A Perfect Star." *Vanity Fair* (January): 112–27.

Connelly, Timothy. 2004. "He Is As He Is – and Always Will Be: Clark Gable and the Reassertion of Hegemonic Masculinity." *The Trouble with Men: Masculinities in European and Hollywood Cinema*. Eds. Phil Powrie et al. London and New York: Wallflower, 34–41.

DeCordova, Richard. 1990. *Picture Personalities: The Emergence of the Star System in America*. Urbana and Chicago: University of Illinois Press.

D'Emilio, John, and Freedman, Estelle B. 1988. *Intimate Matters: A History of Sexuality in America*. New York: Harper & Row.

DiBattista, Maria. 2001. *Fast-Talking Dames*. New Haven and London: Yale University Press.

Dick, Bernard F. 2008. *Claudette Colbert: She Walked in Beauty*. Jackson, MS: University of Mississippi Press.

Doherty, Thomas. 1999. *Pre-Code Hollywood: Sex, Immorality, and Insurrection in American Cinema, 1930–34*. New York: Columbia University Press.

Dyer, Richard. [1979] 1998. *Stars*. London: British Film Institute.

Dyer, Richard. [1986] 2004. *Heavenly Bodies: Film Stars and Society*. 2nd ed. London and New York: Routledge.

Dyer, Richard. 1997. *White*. London and New York: Routledge.

Eckert, Charles. [1978] 1990. "The Carole Lombard in Macy's Window." *Fabrications: Costume and the Female Body*. Ed. Jane Gaines and Charlotte Herzog. New York and London: Routledge, 100–21.

Evans, Peter William, and Deleyto, Celestino. 1998. "Introduction: Surviving Love." *Terms of Endearment: Hollywood Romantic Comedy of the 1980s and*

1990s. Eds. Peter William Evans and Celestino Deleyto. Edinburgh: Edinburgh University Press.

Fisher, Joe. 1993. "Clarke Gable's Balls: Real Men Never Lose Their Teeth." *You Tarzan: Masculinity, Movies and Men.* Ed. Pat Kirkham and Janet Thumim. New York: St. Martin's, 35–51.

Fletcher, Adele Whitely. [1931] 1986. "Marriage à la Colbert." *The Best of Modern Screen.* Ed. Mark Bego. New York: St. Martin's, 166–9.

Freud, Sigmund. 1960. *Jokes and Their Relation to the Unconscious.* Ed. and trans. James Strachey. New York: Norton.

Friedman, Arthur B. [1960] 2004. "Popular Art: Frank Capra." In Poague, 34–69.

Frye, Northrop. 1957. *Anatomy of Criticism: Four Essays.* Princeton, NJ: Princeton University Press.

Gehring, Wes D. 1986. *Screwball Comedy: A Genre of Madcap Romance.* New York, Westport, CT, and London: Greenwood.

Gehring, Wes D. 1995. *Populism and the Capra Legacy.* Westport, CT and London: Greenwood.

Gottlieb, Sidney. 1988. "From Heroine to Brat: Frank Capra's Adaptation of 'Night Bus' (*It Happened One Night*)." *Literature Film Quarterly* 16.2: 129–36.

Gottschalk, Mary. 1995. "AMC's Look at Hollywood Fashion Follows Fads from Screen to Closet." *Pittsburgh Post Gazette* (August 17): C1.

Guglielmo, Thomas A. 2003. " 'No Color Barrier': Italians, Race, and Power in the United States." *Are Italians White? How Race Is Made in America.* Eds. Jennifer Guglielmo and Salvatore Salerno. New York and London: Routledge, 29–43.

Hall, Mordaunt. 1934. "The Screen." *New York Times* (February 23): 23.

Harris, Warren G. 2002. *Clark Gable: A Biography.* New York: Harmony.

Harrison, Paula. [1935] 2004. "The Master of the Human Touch." In Poague, 15–18.

Harvey, James. 1987. *Romantic Comedy in Hollywood, from Lubitch to Sturges.* New York: Knopf.

Haskell, Molly. [1974] 1987. *From Reverence to Rape: The Treatment of Women in the Movies.* 2nd ed. Chicago: University of Chicago Press.

Henderson, Brian. 1986. "Romantic Comedy Today: Semi-Tough or Impossible?" *Film Genre Reader.* Ed. Barry Keith Grant. Austin: University of Texas Press, 309–28.

Heymann, David C. 1983. *Poor Little Rich Girl: The Life and Legend of Barbara Hutton.* New York: Random House.

Jacobs, Lea. 1991. *The Wages of Sin: Censorship and the Fallen Woman Film 1928–1942.* Madison, WI: University of Wisconsin Press.

Jordan, René. 1973. *Clark Gable.* New York: Galahad.

Kendall, Elizabeth. 1990. *The Runaway Bride: Hollywood Romantic Comedy of the 1930s.* New York: Doubleday.

Kyving, David E. 2002. *Daily Life in the United States, 1920–1940*. Chicago: Ivan R. Dee.

Landay, Lori. 1998. *Madcaps, Screwball, and Con Women: The Female Trickster in American Culture*. Philadelphia: University of Pennsylvania Press.

Leff, Leonard J. 1991. "The Breening of America." *Publications of the Modern Language Association* 106: 432–45.

Leff, Leonard J., and Simmons, Jerold L. 1990. *The Dame in the Kimono: Hollywood Censorship and the Production Code from the 1920s to the 1960s*. New York: Grove Weidenfeld.

Lent, Tina Olsin. 1995. "Romantic Love and Friendship: The Redefinition of Gender Relations in Screwball Comedy." *Classical Hollywood Comedy*. Eds. Kristina Karnick and Henry Jenkins. New York: Routledge, 314–31.

Levine, Lawrence. 1985. "Hollywood's Washington: Film Images of National Politics During the Great Depression." *Prospects: An Annual of American Cultural Studies*. Ed. Jack Salzman. New York: Cambridge University Press, 169–95.

Maddox, Ben. 1970. "What about Clark Gable Now?" *Hollywood and the Great Fan Magazines*. Ed. Martin Levin. New York: Random House, 20–1, 173–4.

Maland, Charles. 1995. *Frank Capra*. New York: Twayne.

Maltby, Richard. 1998. "*It Happened One Night*: The Recreation of the Patriarch." In Sklar and Zagarrio 1998b, 130–63.

Mann, William J. 2001. *Behind the Scenes: How Gays and Lesbians Shaped Hollywood 1910–1969*. New York: Viking.

McBride, Joseph. 1992. *Frank Capra: The Catastrophe of Success*. New York: Simon & Schuster.

McDonald, Tamar Jeffers. 2007. *Romantic Comedy: Boy Meets Girl Genre*. London and New York: Wallflower.

McElvaine, Robert S. 1993. *The Great Depression: America, 1929–41*. New York: Times Books.

Mayne, Judith. 1993. *Cinema and Spectatorship*. London and New York: Routledge.

Mizejewski, Linda. 2007. "Queen Latifah, Unruly Women, and the Bodies of Romantic Comedy." *Genders* 46. Available at www.genders.org/g46/g46_mizejewski.html (accessed March 27, 2009).

Mosher, John. 1934. "The Current Cinema." *New Yorker* (March 3): 58–9.

Motion Picture Production Code. 1930. Available at www.artsreformation.com/a001/hays-code.html (accessed March 27, 2009).

Muscio, Giuliana. 1998. "Roosevelt, Arnold, and Capra, (or) the Federalist–Populist Paradox." In Sklar and Zagarrio 1998b, 164–89.

Neale, Steve, and Krutnik, Frank. 1990. *Popular Film and Television Comedy*. New York and London: Routledge.

Norton, Helen B. 1934. "Fun on a Night Bus." *Vanity Fair* (April): 50.

Orgeron, Marsha. 2003. "Making *It* in Hollywood: Clara Bow, Fandom, and Consumer Culture." *Cinema Journal* 42.4: 76–97.

Parish, James Robert. 1972. *The Paramount Pretties*. New York: Castle.

Pennington, Jody W. 2007. *The History of Sex in American Film*. Westport, CT and London: Praeger.

Poague, Leland. 1975. *The Cinema of Frank Capra: An Approach to Film Comedy*. South Brunswick and New York: A. S. Barnes/London: Tantivy.

Poague, Leland. 1977. "*As You Like It* and *It Happened One Night*: The Generic Pattern of Comedy." *Literature/Film Quarterly* 5: 346–50.

Poague, Leland. 1994. *Another Frank Capra*. New York: Cambridge University Press.

Poague, Leland, ed. 2004. *Frank Capra Interviews*. Jackson, MS: University Press of Mississippi.

Preston, Catherine. 2000. "Hanging on a Star: The Resurrection of the Romance Film in the 1990s." *Film Genre 2000: New Critical Essays*. Ed. Wheeler Winston Dixon. Albany: State University of New York Press, 227–43.

Quirck, Lawrence J. 1985. *Claudette Colbert: An Illustrated Biography*. New York: Crown.

Richards, Jeffrey. [1970] 1976. "Frank Capra and the Cinema of Populism." *Movies and Methods*. Ed. Bill Nichols. Berkeley and Los Angeles: University of California Press, 65–77.

Rowe, Kathleen. 1995. *The Unruly Woman: Gender and the Genres of Laughter*. Austin: University of Texas Press.

Rush, George, and Molloy, Joanna. 1996. "It Happened One Night – Or Did It?" *New York Daily News* (August 5): 14.

Russo, Vito. 1987. *The Celluloid Closet: Homosexuality in the Movies*. Rev. ed. New York: Harper & Row.

Schatz, Thomas. 1981. *Hollywood Genres: Formulas, Filmmaking, and the Studio System*. New York: Random House.

Schatz, Thomas. 1998. "Anatomy of a House Director: Capra, Cohn, and Columbia in the 1930s." In Sklar and Zagarrio 1998b, 10–36.

Shumway, David R. 2003. *Modern Love: Romance, Intimacy, and the Marriage Crisis*. New York and London: New York University Press.

Sikov, Ed. 1989. *Screwball: America's Madcap Romantic Comedies*. New York: Crown.

Sklar, Robert. 1975. *Movie-Made America: A Cultural History of American Movies*. New York: Random House.

Sklar, Robert. 1998. "A Leap into the Void: Frank Capra's Apprenticeship to Ideology." In Sklar and Zagarrio 1998b, 37–63.

Sklar, Robert, and Zagarrio, Vito. 1998a. "Introduction." In Sklar and Zagarrio 1998b, 1–9.

Sklar, Robert, and Zagarrio, Vito, eds. 1998b. *Frank Capra: Authorship and the Studio System*. Philadelphia: Temple University Press.

Smoodin, Eric. 2004. *Regarding Frank Capra: Audience, Celebrity and American Film Studies 1930–1960*. Durham, NC and London: Duke University Press.

Spicer, Chrystopher J. 2002. *Clark Gable: Biography, Filmography, Bibliography*. Jefferson, NC and London: McFarland.

Tapert, Annette. 1998. *The Power of Glamour: The Women who Defined the Magic of Stardom*. New York: Crown.

Taves, Brian. 1998. "Studio Metamorphosis: Columbia's Emergence from Poverty Row." In Sklar and Zagarrio 1998b, 222–54.

Troy, William. 1934. "Picaresque." *Nation* (March 14): 314.

Troy, William. 1940. "On a Classic." *Nation* (April 10): 426–7.

Urban Legends. 2007. "The Shirt Off His Back." Available at www.snopes.com/movies/actors/gable1.asp (accessed March 27, 2009).

Van Rensselaer, Philip. 1979. *Million Dollar Baby: An Intimate Portrait of Barbara Hutton*. New York: Putnam.

Variety. 1934. Review of *It Happened One Night*. *Variety* (February 27). Available at www.variety.com/index.asp?layout=Variety100&reviewid=VE1117792058&content=jump&jump=review&category=1935&cs=1 (accessed March 27, 2009).

Walker, Alexander. 1970. *Stardom: The Hollywood Phenomenon*. New York: Stein & Day.

Watts, Richard, Jr. 1934. "On the Screen." *New York Herald Tribune* (February 23): 14.

Williams, Chester. 1968. *Gable*. New York: Fleet.

Wood, Michael. 1975. *America in the Movies*. New York: Columbia University Press.

Young, Kay. 1994. "Hollywood, 1934: 'Inventing' Romantic Comedy." *Look Who's Laughing: Gender and Comedy*. Ed. Gail Finney. Langhorne, PA: Gordon & Breach, 257–74.

Index

The Palm Beach Story (1942), 121
Paramount Pictures, 12, 110–13,
    116–17
Pasadena, 11
patriarchy, 38, 66, 70, 108, 119
Payne Study and Experiment Fund,
    46, 49
Pennington, Joey, 45
The Philadelphia Story (1940), 18
Pickford, Mary, 44
Pillow Talk (1959), 18
Poague, Leland, 39, 123 n.4, 124 n.5
populism, 84–6, 123 nn. 4, 5. *See also*
    Capra, Frank
Possessed (1931), 101
Pressman, Joel, 114
Production Code, *see* Motion Picture
    Production Code of 1930
Production Code Administration, 46
The Public Enemy (1931), 100
Puccini for Beginners (2006), 18
The Purple Rose of Cairo (1985), 74

Quirck, Lawrence J., 112–13

race, 87–9, 115, 117, 124 n.6
Red Dust (1932), 101
Richards, Jeffrey, 84, 86
Riskin, Robert, 9, 14–15, 89, 102, 112,
    116–17
RKO, 12
Rogen, Seth, 115
Rogers, Ginger, 74
Rogers, Will, 75
romantic comedy, 2–4, 15, 42, 75, 82,
    102, 109, 121, 122 n.2
    anti-authoritarian spirit of, 94
    battle of the sexes in, 52, 104
    and class, 83
    and the comic delay of sex, 47
    during the Depression, 70

dialogue in, 60–1, 64
formula and history of, 17–21, 34
heroine of, 19–20, 112, 115, 117–18
as heterosexuality's most widely
    circulated story, 115
importance for women, 19–20,
    32–3, 38–9, 112
and marriage, 38–9, 62–3, 120–1
"meet cute" device, 21–2
romanticism, 6
Roosevelt, Franklin Delano, 72,
    86, 88
Rowe, Kathleen, 9, 19–20, 35, 38, 41,
    62–3, 66, 77, 83, 93–4, 118, 121
Rubinstein, Helena, 74
Runaway Bride (1999), 121
Russian Revolution, 72
Russo, Vito, 43

Scandal Sheet (1931), 10
Schatz, Thomas, 28, 83
screwball comedy, 21–2, 24, 29, 32, 34,
    38, 61, 75, 97, 122 n.2. *See also*
    romantic comedy
The Sea Cloud (yacht), 79
sex and sexuality, 2, 5–6, 15–17, 20, 34,
    37, 61, 97
    and censorship, 41–2, 45, 67
    changes in attitudes during the
        1920s, 44, 48–9
    and Clark Gable, 99–100
    and Claudette Colbert, 112
    cultural representations of, 9, 59
    Foucault's theory of, 47, 59, 115
    and jokes, 58
Shakespeare, William, 10, 18–20, 67,
    94–5, 118
Shapeley, Oscar, 33, 52, 85, 103–4
Shaw, George Bernard, 20
Shearer, Norma, 99–100
She Married Her Boss (1935), 12